"Terry Esau's voice as he scouts for evidence of the Almighty is casual and generous, sometimes skipping to the deep end of the pool when we least expect it. *Surprise Me* is a reminder not merely to pray but to watch for (and enjoy) the unpredictable answer."

— LEIF ENGER
author of *Peace Like a River*

"In this gem of a book, Terry Esau writes with wit, humor, and grace about the little miracles of connection and complication we all encounter daily and hourly. I commend the book and the Surprise Me experiment to anyone who wants to shake up his or her spiritual life for the better."

— GREG GARRETT
author of *Free Bird* and *Holy Superheros!*

"In Terry Esau's *Surprise Me*, we see that the Christian experience is not so much about fancy theological arguments as it is about a day-to-day life vibrantly finger-painted by the joyful hand of God."

— IAN PUNNETT
MDiv, radio talk show host

"Candor, warm wit, and insight abound as fellow sojourner Terry Esau chronicles his personal epiphanic test-drive of present-moment living. *Surprise Me* invites each of us to discover the heart of what it means to practice the presence of God. Yesterday is gone. Tomorrow has not yet come. Today is here. God is in every moment, right now."

— KARLA YACONELLI
owner/CEO, Youth Specialties

"On this quest, Terry discovers God between the frames of a movie, in the sleeping breaths of our spouses, and on the holy land that constitutes the street where we live. He didn't find the Lord of gilded chariots and fiery glory but rather the artisan of everyday life."

— JOHN OLSON
president, Olson and Company, Brand Champions

"If you want to read something fresh and new — and enjoy every minute of the journey — you need to grab this book! My friends often joke that I write more books than I read, but this book is more than enough reason to leave my computer and turn some great pages!"

—STEVE GOTTRY
coauthor (with Ken Blanchard) of *The On-Time, On-Target Manager*,
author of *Common Sense Business*

"*Surprise Me* is an invitation to an open-eyed, optimistic life with God. Terry Esau uses his unique perspective in creating an irresistible invitation to live with God in the here and now. This is a wonderful book."

—DOUG PAGITT
pastor; author of *BodyPrayer*

"*Surprise Me* is a simple wake-up-and-live, non-formulaic exercise in spending our days with God. This is a good read — and an even better way to live."

—GREGG STEINHAFEL,
president, Target Corporation

"The spiritual life is first about seeing — and seeing well. This book will teach you to do that in most ordinary and exciting ways. Once you learn how to see, you will know God for yourself and not just believe!"

—RICHARD ROHR
O.F.M., Center for Action and Contemplation

"You stole my thoughts."

—REID BRADLEY
college student

"This book is not what I expected. It's about everyday life and how God meets us there — or maybe we meet him, I don't know. All I do know is that I will never be able to look at another day as being simply "ordinary." This book hit me between the eyes. But then again, knowing Terry, that really doesn't Surprise Me."

—NEAL JOSEPH
executive pastor, Fellowship Bible Church, Brentwood, Tennessee

SURPRISE ME

A 30-DAY FAITH EXPERIMENT

TERRY ESAU

NAVPRESS®

BRINGING TRUTH TO LIFE

The Navigators is an international Christian organization. Our mission is to reach, disciple, and equip people to know Christ and to make Him known through successive generations. We envision multitudes of diverse people in the United States and every other nation who have a passionate love for Christ, live a lifestyle of sharing Christ's love, and multiply spiritual laborers among those without Christ.

NavPress is the publishing ministry of The Navigators. NavPress publications help believers learn biblical truth and apply what they learn to their lives and ministries. Our mission is to stimulate spiritual formation among our readers.

© 2005 by Terry Esau

ISBN 1-57683-823-4

Cover design by Disciple Design
Cover photograph by Getty Images
Creative Team: Terry Behimer, Steve Parolini, Darla Hightower, Arvid Wallen, Glynese Northam

Some of the anecdotal illustrations in this book are true to life and are included with the permission of the persons involved. All other illustrations are composites of real situations, and any resemblance to people living or dead is coincidental.

Esau, Terry, 1954-
Surprise me : a 30-day faith experiment / Terry Esau.-- 1st ed.
   p. cm.
ISBN 1-57683-823-4 (alk. paper)
1. Trust in God. 2. Spiritual life--Christianity. I. Title.
BV4637.E83 2005
242'.2--dc22

2005009063

Printed in the Canada

1 2 3 4 5 6 7 8 9 10 / 09 08 07 06 05

To Brian

The son I never had and the soul mate Brianna has longed for.

Welcome to the family.

Oh, and thanks for saving me from purse shopping.

CONTENTS

Acknowledgments 9

Reality Spirituality 11

Day One: Fleeced 15

Day Two: The Ride 23

Day Three: Floating 30

Day Four: Cow Pies 35

Day Five: Rules of Punctuation 40

Day Six: Agenda Saboteurs 44

Day Seven: Taxi Driver 49

Day Eight: Lessons from Pam 53

Day Nine: The Purse Skirmish 61

Day Ten: A Christmas Story 68

Day Eleven: Dispensing Hope 75

Day Twelve: The Wah-Wah/Fuzz Pedal 81

Day Thirteen: Change Everything 87

Day Fourteen: ShoeBob 93

Day Fifteen: Taylor's Song 99

Day Sixteen: The Party 107

Day Seventeen: Midnight Blue 113

Day Eighteen: Kitchen Conversation 119

Day Nineteen: Raining Boxsters 124

Day Twenty: Bronco Busting 131

Day Twenty-One: Standby 137

Day Twenty-Two: Mattress Shopping 142

Day Twenty-Three: No TV? 147

Day Twenty-Four: Window Shopping 152

Day Twenty-Five: Counting Surprises 158

Day Twenty-Six: Stepford Christians 163

Day Twenty-Seven: All or Nothing 168

Day Twenty-Eight: A Love Supreme 174

Day Twenty-Nine: Four Guys 179

Day Thirty/AM: Construction Barrel 186

Day Thirty/PM: Three Songs 192

Author 201

ACKNOWLEDGMENTS

To Mary — my wife, my Ado Annie, my Love Supreme. You know me like no one on the planet . . . and still, you love me.

To Brianna — who slept on my chest the first day of her life as I watched Superbowl XVI. You left a permanent indentation on my heart that day.

To Lauren — you've grown up and moved, but my heart's still in denial about it. Your voice, when you call me "Dad," is one of the sweetest sounds I know.

To Taylor — my Tator Tot, who I hold onto a little too tightly. If I squeeze you too hard it's because I love you too much.

These four women have stolen and subdivided my heart — I never want it back, or put together.

To the Esaus and the Soholts — families by any other name could not be as sweet. I love you all.

To all of my dear friends — you are scattered throughout this book (mostly with fabricated names) and sprinkled through my life. You mean the world to me. Mary and I are rich in one area far more than any other, and that's in friendships. Our stockpiled relational wealth makes Donald Trump's riches seem paltry. You are the joy to us that money could never buy.

To Terry Behimer from NavPress — who was captured by this concept almost before I presented it. It seemed you were waiting, looking for this idea. Thank you.

To Steve Parolini, my editor, who I now call friend. You debunked my grammar that weren't so good, elucidated my metaphorical mumbo-jumbo, and demystified my dyslexic ramblings—all the while entertaining me. (Personally, I don't know what the dig beal is with dyslexia. It boesn't dother me at all.)

To all the other great people at NavPress—you're my heroes, and I am so grateful for what you have already done and continue to do.

To Ann, the postmaster in Mart, Texas—don't hate me.

To Mart, Texas—ditto.

To the idiot in the red car who ran me off the road and into a construction barrel, but more importantly he ran me into a relationship with Norm. You meant it for bad, but it all came out good.

To John Coltrane, Rogers and Hammerstein, and whoever wrote that stupid song I can't get out of my head, "Window Shopping."

To inanimate objects that smuggle holy water into my understanding—like mattresses, wah-wah/fuzz pedals, umbrellas, purses, and fleeces.

To Kirkpatrick Macmillan for inventing the bicycle—this vehicle has carried me into many surprising "circumstances." I'm beginning to view it as a mode of spiritual transportation.

To the colleges, churches, small groups, and book clubs around the country that have already engaged in this Surprise Me experiment. God bless you guinea pigs!

To change that won't let me settle.

To pain that reminds me to feel.

To life that's crammed with surprise.

And lastly, to my partner—the guy who drives the red Gran Torino. See you in my driveway—tomorrow morning.

REALITY SPIRITUALITY

And on the eighth day God said, "Surprise!"

I was watching some reality TV the other day. Weird stuff. I get the impression they want me to think that I'm eavesdropping on an adventure — that it's spontaneous, unscripted, raw, real, alive. Well, Gilbert and Carol didn't raise the brightest boy, but even I'm not that gullible.

Still, it got me thinking. What would a Reality TV show look like if it was about our faith? You know, Reality Spirituality. I suppose there would be several forms of competition.

Maybe the show would open with *The Parking Prayer Competition*. Contestants would be deposited in large SUVs, probably white Hummers plastered with sponsorship logos, about a mile from the mall. Then they'd be given thirty seconds to pray and ask God for a really good parking place. Whoever got a spot closest to the entrance would be declared the winner.

Or maybe they'd have a *Restaurant Prayer Competition*. Contestants would get extra points for longest prayer and loudest volume and could earn bonus points if they got the entire clientele, including the waitstaff, to bow their heads.

I have a few other ideas as well, but it only gets worse from here. Let's just say I hope that show never makes it to TV. If you have to go on TV to prove how spiritual you are, haven't you just disproven it? Our faith is not a competition.

Yet, there's something intriguing about an aspect of this — the reality part. Wouldn't it be cool if our faith were a little more raw, a little more real, more spontaneous, unscripted, more like an adventure?

So I got this idea, not for a TV show but an experiment. A faith experiment.

Thirty Days — A three-word prayer — A trail of surprises

What if:

Every day, for thirty days, I pray and ask God to surprise me? "Surprise Me, God." Nothing more, nothing less. Three words. Not asking for something in particular. Not giving him my list. Not presenting my agenda. Just inviting him to barge into my life in any old way he pleases — to crash into the busyness of my schedule and mess with it.

Then, what if:

Every day I record my thoughts and activities? All the twists and turns that give shape to the month. I'll look for when, where, and how God steps into my world in a practical, everyman sort of way, and then I'll transfer it all onto my hard drive. I suspect this won't be a collection of "highlight" stories (TV tales of only the positively answered prayers that seem out of context and too good to be believed), but rather a measure of "reality spirituality." I suspect it will include stories of seemingly unanswered prayers as well. Maybe the surprise will be that on many days no sugarcoated coincidences aligned at all — the day headed south and just kept going. Maybe the surprise will be in how I handle that, or don't handle it. Maybe the surprises will be more internal than external. Maybe the sea will part, the rod will bud, and the sky will rain biscuits. Maybe not.

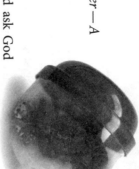

I have no idea what those "maybes" will look like — except that I expect they won't be what I expect. Today there is no story. I'll be done. The book of stories will have been written, assisted by the Surprise-Meister. All the "aha" moments will be in the bag; the good, the bad, and probably the odd as well.

I'm hoping it will be a tapestry that blends my physical, emotional, and spiritual worlds. I'm hoping it will feel real and honest. I'm hoping it *won't* feel like one of those happily-ever-after, dimple-grinned Christian tomes that smack of well-intentioned inauthenticity. I'm hoping it will look like thirty days in the life of a regular guy who embarked on a terribly irregular experiment.

I'm not exactly sure why I'm doing this, except that I feel the need to stir the pot of my personal suburban faith. Maybe this is a plea for an adrenalin shot-to-the-heart for the sake of my spiritual resuscitation. I want to see and hear strong beeps on my spiritual heart-rate-monitor. I want to live large.

I'm a little nervous. I like control, always have. This is yielding the paintbrush. It's saying, "Okay, I'll be your canvas for a month. Paint away. Any color. Any subject. Trowel, paint gun, or brush. Have at me!"

Well — here goes.

"Surprise Me, God!"

DAY ONE: FLEECED

Well, this is it. This first day of the "experiment." It feels kind of weird, like I've started a game and I don't know the rules. I don't know how to play. I'm not even sure of the goal. It's like I'm on a scavenger hunt, but nobody gave me the list.

I've got to tell you, part of me feels an odd sort of pressure to come up with the goods. You know, extraordinary stories of miraculous events—the kind they make miniseries about or air on PAX TV. What if nothing like that happens? What if this ends up being the dullest month of my life? Who's going to want to read that? Will that make God look bad? Will it make *me* look bad? Is this whole idea stupid? Maybe this whole idea is just the unfortunate result of eating bad chicken.

I wish my ideas came with a logbook that clearly identified their source. "This one's from God, this one—not so much." It would make things so much easier. It does make me wonder . . . is God anti-easy? I suppose he just wants me to use my brain. And I guess if he robbed me of that option I'd be whining all the more.

Sorry. This is supposed to be a record of my days and the events that happen in those days. Not my disjointed mental meanderings. Maybe this experiment will be more about the processing and understanding of life than the actual chronological documentation of it. Hmm.

Enough conundruming.

Woke up at 4 a.m. I wouldn't call that a surprise, at least not a pleasant one. Trust me, I didn't set the alarm for four bells. I think it was the anticipation of this day. The subconscious wheels were cruising when they should have been snoozing. I hate that.

Got up, showered. Walked Bailey, our English Springer Spaniel. She didn't seem to notice anything special in the day. Just did her business in a very rote sort of way.

When I got back home, I did a little reading and had some toast while Katie Couric yammered on in the background. The starting line for the experiment was staring at me. Maybe I should stretch a bit more before I step up to the line. I was . . . um . . . *surprised* to find myself a bit hesitant to actually say those words, "Surprise Me, God." Once I say them for the first time, the game is on. The game without rules.

As I was eating I started thinking about the story of Gideon in the Bible. Remember how he was testing God's direction by putting a fleece out at night? He said, "Okay, if this is what you want me to do, tomorrow morning let the fleece be dry and the ground around it be wet." It was. And then, another test. "Okay, that was pretty good, God. Now, let the fleece be wet and the ground be dry. Then I'll know this is you, Mr. Anti-Easy, directing me."

Jump ahead a few thousand years. It's the inaugural Surprise Me day. Maybe I should have put out a fleece to make sure this was a Really Good Idea. Or am *I* the fleece? I don't think I'm testing God to see if this or that direction is true and from him, like Gideon. But I may be testing myself to see if I can hold water, holy water. I wonder if this whole thing is more about my ability, or my willingness to soak up the rain he causes to fall on me. Maybe it's about throwing away my umbrella, getting rid of the protections and distractions that keep me from seeing what God wants to dump into my life.

Can I hold the surprises he rains on me?

I walked out our back door onto the deck. I looked up at our bedroom windows to see if Mary was still sleeping. *Zzzzz.* Then I did something a bit odd — at least it felt odd. I lay down on the deck, flopped my arms out wide, and looked up at the clouds. Bailey threw me a "what's-he-up-to-now" glance.

I took a deep breath, then said, "God, here's your fleece. Soak me." I followed my request with those three words he'd better get used to:

"Surprise Me, God."

I lay there for a few seconds. The wind blew, the birds chirped. There was no Terry-as-target bolt of lightning. Nor did I suddenly receive the supernatural ability to see into the future or cure acne or rattle off the names of the riders in the 1938 Tour de France in alphabetical order.

Life was copacetic.

I got up and dusted myself off, making sure that my back was cleared of leaves, twigs, and other deck crud. How would I explain the outdoor-living collage on my back to my wife? What would I say? "Uh, little dust storm kicked up out there, blew a bunch of debris onto my, uh, back. Weirdest thing." She already looks at me sideways. I don't want her to reconsider institutionalizing me.

It felt good to be underway.

Interesting thing about this experiment — it's not taking place in a vacuum. I'm not taking time off to do it. I haven't set aside thirty days to laboratory-ize it. Life as I know it will continue, and this project will weave itself in and around and through it. That is intentional. I want this to be a slice of the normal life I lead, not a scripted event that doesn't relate to my everyday existence. Surprise Me is about inviting God into my life *as is*.

My life *as is* continued at a meeting with our church staff to present this Surprise Me idea. I had mentioned it to our pastor the week earlier over coffee. His ears perked up like Bailey's as I was telling him how it worked, and he asked me to come and present it to the staff. I did. It went well. They decided to use it as the fall kick-off campaign at our church.

Four Sundays, five Wednesdays. We'll get the whole church engaged in this experiment. On the first Sunday we're going to introduce the idea and hand everyone a thirty-day journal. Then, on Wednesdays during our whole-church gathering, we'll recap the past week's Surprises and break into the already existing small groups for everyone to tell their stories. I think this is going to be a good thing. Think of the community—the bonding that will take place as people tell their stories of God working in their lives. How can this not be fun?

After I returned home, I had a conference call with a radio station in Florida. I'm composing a new package of image music for their station. Did I mention that I'm in the music business? I mostly write and produce music for TV commercials, but I also score documentary films, TV show themes, TV news packages, radio commercials, and radio station campaigns. I used to own a full-blown recording studio until a year ago. It was a pretty cool space, occupying a 100-year-old bank building of rough brick, huge windows, high ceilings—and had an atmosphere that rocked. I gave it a name: The Coast. This was my creative home for the past seventeen years. Some days I miss it.

When I sold The Coast I decided to turn the space above our garages into a much smaller home studio. If it hadn't turned out so cool, I think I'd miss The Coast even more, but my new digs feel so right—like my new creative home.

So I'm sitting in my new space, calling this radio station in Florida. I had e-mailed seven or eight music files to them, and this was the "We like it/We hate it" conference call. I don't worry about these meetings like I did in the early days. Long ago I realized that I can't predict someone's musical tastes or preferences. They skew toward the randomly illogical. And when you get a group of people on the phone and try to come to a consensus, well, does the phrase "when hell freezes over" mean anything to you?

Evidently it was a cooler day than normal in hell — they liked, and agreed to, almost all of it. Gotta like those subterranean cold fronts. They wanted a few changes, but nothing with meteorological significance.

After the phone call I had to cruise to a lunch meeting. I met with Mark, a guy who leads worship at his church. He just wanted to talk about life, dreams, vision, and stuff like that. He's one of those people who will do something really new, really groundbreaking one day. I encourage people like that to do it, just flat out do it. "Incrementalism is innovation's worst enemy." I don't know who said that, but I love this phrase and think it's packed with a lot of truth. We're always trying to ease our way into change — *same* our way into something different. We try to do it in such a way that nobody feels uncomfortable. Long ago I decided that in my music business, if everybody feels good and safe with the music, then it must be weak, impotent, passionless. And it probably won't achieve its purpose. I call this the S & T factor. If there's not at least one person who Squirms and Twitches when they hear it, then toss it out, it's dead.

I encouraged Mark to innovate even if there were some S & T-ers in the crowd. Don't you think we need to start swinging art a bit more like a sword? I encouraged Mark to pull his ideas from the scabbard and slice away at some stale air. Hope he doesn't get in trouble. Or he may come looking for me with a more-than-metaphorical sword.

Mark told me at lunch about a mutual friend of ours, Bruce, who quit his job and is looking to start an experience-based café — a place where art would be used to gently poke and prod people to think and talk about life, love, faith, and God. Now that's a sword-worthy idea. It's always pleasantly surprising to hear about people like that. I wish they were the norm instead of the extremely remote exception.

In my first book I wrote a story about a café . . . sort of. It was actually about a bar called The Church. God was the sole proprietor of the joint, not to mention the bartender. (Yes, it was all metaphorical.) The people who showed up at The Church were as diverse and as uniquely strange as are the people who show up in church every Sunday. And the drink selections represented the variety of choices those people make. God had his own "special concoction" that he offered everybody, but few took it.

Happy hour would be a lot happier if we'd all just wise up and drink his drink. Anyhow, it's an interesting premise. Read the story and then come to Minneapolis and check out Bruce's new café. Who says we don't have modern-day samurais?

Home from lunch, which always lasts longer than lunches have a right to, I started putting together the proposal for this Surprise Me idea (it's not yet a book). My intent was to finish preparing the proposal and send it to several publishers. At this point in the experiment, I have to admit I'm not even sure this thing would work as a book. But the idea keeps stalking me.

I didn't finish the proposal. And you don't want to send a half-cooked idea to a publisher. Book Ideas Tartare don't make it out of the concept kitchen. I'll finish it up tomorrow and FedEx it.

As I'm writing all of this I'm thinking, none of this is surprising. I'm just writing a boring travelogue on the unexciting life of some guy you've only just met (well, except those of you who are relatives and friends and have been kind enough to buy this book even though I probably should have given you one for free).

But this is just Day One. Wing it with me for a few days and things may get interesting. Or not. I guess we'll be surprised together.

Mary, my beautiful wife and chief surprise dispenser of the last quarter century, was working today, so it was just me and two of our three daughters, Taylor and Lauren, for dinner. I make some mean chili, killer breakfasts, and Surprise Me-Smoothies, but other than that I'm a cooking illiterate. So rather than subjecting my loving daughters to a blendered meal of green beans, Rotelle, hazelnut yogurt, mushrooms, and three shakes of Bacos (I love a little crunch in my smoothies), we decided to go to Retro, a just-opened coffee shop café. Taylor invited her buddy Alex to join us and we were off.

Taylor is our fifteen-year-old, almost sixteen — though she seems almost twenty. She's all that and a bag of chips. Her friend Alex is all that and a bag of B-B-Q chips. The two of them together produce some serious crunch. Lauren is our middle daughter, twenty, a sophomore at Baylor University in Texas, home for the summer working as a server at Italiani's Restaurant. How would I describe her? Maybe a chili pepper in a bowl of Malt-o-Meal. It's not that she's all spicy in a puddle of blah, she just does her own thing, has her own opinions, and walks them down the road with a subtle confidence. I've also seen her be the dollop of Malt-o-Meal in a steaming bowl of jalapenos.

Sitting, eating, and talking with my girls, including Alex, is on my "top three things I love in life" list. We talked at length with one of the owners as we were ordering. There are railroad tracks just twenty feet from the restaurant. Heidi, the owner, told us that sometimes the engineers will call in their order ahead of time, then stop the train by the drive-through window to pick up some bean before choo-chooing off into the distance. Who's ever heard of a drive-through window for Burlington Northerns? That right there has got to make you love this place.

As we were leaving, Tay took a job application from Heidi. She's thinking about becoming a bean-brew-schlepper, part-time. I can hear her now, "That's three dark roasts, a mocha frappacino, and a latte with skim-no whip for the guy in the caboose. That'll be $13.26. Please chug up to the window."

I dropped the girls off at home and then ran by the high school to catch the second half of a soccer game. I know a bunch of the guys on this college-age men's team, so it's fun to watch. Besides, when soccer is played the way it's supposed to be played, it is, without a doubt, the beautiful game. It's amazing to watch, the anticipation, the unity, the effort, the vision.

I couldn't help but think, "If we as human beings could learn to work together like this, the world would certainly be a better place." When a player dribbling the ball downfield is pressured by the defense, his teammate behind him yells, "support," and the guy dribbling drops the ball back to him. They maintain control. On a good soccer team, the player with the ball never tries to do more than he could or should. And his teammates are always looking out for him — recognizing trouble and letting him know about it. They trust each other. And sometimes — often, even — they move the ball forward by temporarily going backward. Soccer is all about the greater good, not the individual performance.

Wouldn't it be cool if churches were more like soccer teams?

Well, that's day one. As I walked Bailey I thought back over the day. It was what it was. No big surprises. No page-turning thrills. Not many scientific journals are page-turners, either. Just the same, I'm hoping that this doesn't read too scientifically. I guess it's not really up to me. Or is it? This is supposed to be a journal of the God-moments in my life, but if I'm a dull-eyed dimwit I won't see them. And maybe that's the first surprise after all — a God-reminder that I need to keep my eyes open and not let life become a forgettable blur.

It's late. Thanks for reading day one. And God, thanks for letting me play fleece-man today. Do you mind if I do it again tomorrow? I felt a few droplets that I think were from you.

Send more.

DAY TWO: THE RIDE

If life is a giant Hide-and-Seek-athon, wouldn't you assume that God is the hider and we are the seekers? That always seemed like a safe assumption to me. I'm not so sure anymore. What if we're the hiders, and God is poking around shrubs, sniffing under rocks and behind garbage cans looking for anyone who wants to be found. It does track with that whole shepherd and lost sheep thing he talked about.

I think I may have seen him sniffing around my yard today.

The day started rather inconsequentially, as most of my days do. *Woke up, got outta bed, dragged a comb across my head* . . . I had a bunch of stuff to do today, not the least of which was to FedEx the proposal for this very book idea to several publishers. I had to write cover letters, make copies (I love Kinkos, and Kinkos loves me), stuff, address, paperclip, lick, rip, tear, and send e-mails. E-mails that hyped the coming proposal and said,

Hey, you got a shocker coming in your P.O. box tomorrow, Mr. Publisher dude. Don't miss it. It's the surprise you've been looking for!

I was trying to convey my passion, but sometimes passion and pitch are like identical twins. I can't tell them apart — and I birthed them.

So that process had me twitching. Then I had to take Lauren (our middle daughter, you met her yesterday) to work because one of our cars came up limping. I may not have mentioned the car thing as a valid

23

surprise because I fully expect it to come up lame every day. It's a Land Rover Discovery . . . of the older variety. Predisposed to decompose. And resuscitating those dinosaurs is a piggy bank buster.

I dropped her off at the restaurant where she works, then headed to a brainstorming meeting for a community-wide multi-church gathering event. No real surprises at the meeting except this one idea we came up with that I thought was pretty cool: Have the pastor from one church stand and say what he loves about the pastor from another church—what he's learned from him, why he believes in what they're doing at the other church, and so on. You know, bragging about the "competitor." We thought that would be a great way to set an example for the people. A "we're-all-on-the-same-team" sort of talk.

We all came away feeling like we made progress . . . and we got a good, *free*, Italian lunch. *Mmmmm*, farfalle with artichokes and shrimp followed by cantucci di prato. *Bellissima*. Then I picked up Lauren from work. The poor kid had slaved away for three straight hours and was wearing alfredo sauce on her shirt.

Back home I finished with the e-mails and packages and shuttled the latter to the FedEx box, where they magically disappeared only to materialize the next day in the hands of terribly excited publishers.

By this time it was 4:39 p.m. I considered starting another project, but opted for my favorite distraction instead—a bike ride. Bicycle, that is. The self-powered variety. The kind that makes you sweat. I think we were made to sweat, cuz for some reason sweating makes me happy.

I can't even tell you how much I love riding my bicycle. I fell in love with this a few years back—after I tore the ACL in my knee playing basketball, and after I tore my Achilles tendon playing basketball, and after I tore my calf muscle playing soccer. (I'm about as reliable as my Rover. Predisposed to decompose.) Essentially I had nothing left, athletically speaking, except bike riding. At first I was depressed about that, but then

I discovered bicycle *racing*. Presto = Buono. Speed = Good.

Now I'm one of those weekend warriors who wears "wind-cheater" spandex (much to the dismay and embarrassment of my daughters), rides a bike that costs more than my car, and is passionate about . . . okay, obsessed and addicted to the whole thing.

This weekend is the State Championship Criterium race, so I've been training like a Lance Armstrong-wannabe. We had a party to go to at 7 p.m., but it was only 4:39. That left plenty of time to thoroughly trash myself—to see if I can get my heart rate up to 180 without infarcting my cardio. I hopped on my "two-wheeled carbon-fibered aerodynamic second mortgage" and went out to kick some asphalt.

Less than a mile from my house I pull up behind a guy who wasn't moving very fast. Guess he's not training for the State Crit race. I figured to just blow by him, maybe say hi, but that's it. As I got to his back wheel, I thought about the "Surprise Me, God" prayer I prayed this morning. "Oh geez (that's how we Minnesotans curse), do I have to talk to him? Okay, but just long enough to find out if he's a 'player' in this Surprise Me game. I'll give him fifteen feet. If he doesn't say something 'surprising,' I'm gone."

We made small talk for ten feet. At fourteen feet I found out he'd just returned from climbing Mt. McKinley in Alaska. Interesting. "Okay, I'll give him fifteen feet more." I told him I've seen all the great mountain-climbing disaster movies—avalanches, blizzards, you know. He didn't say much. In fact he changed the subject.

He asked me a bunch of questions about who I am, what I do—standard fare for two guys. I talked about my music studio and my recent decision to sell it and try other things.

"What other things?" he asked.

"Well, I wrote a book."

"About what?"

"Well, about God and who he is and who we are and how we fit together, at least how we try to." I told him it's a bunch of short stories, metaphorical pictures of this God. I couldn't really tell if he was interested or not.

So then he asked, "What are you working on now?"

I told him I'm two days into a spiritual experiment. "Every day I pray, 'Surprise Me, God.' Then I wait to see what happens and write it down. I think it's going to be pretty interesting."

There was a long pause, and then he looked over at me and said, "You want to be surprised?" I thought, okay, another mile won't kill my conditioning. Besides, he had me curious.

"My buddy was killed on McKinley." He took a breath. "He got caught in a rock slide. Didn't make it. I'm having a hard time knowing what to do with this." There were pauses between thoughts. He seemed to be struggling to find the words. "I took the day off work today to do some thinking."

He went on to tell me about the climb—which had become a nearly three-week expedition because of bad weather. On the ascent, a blizzard sent him and his buddy into their tent for four days and nights, periodically digging out to keep from getting buried. He told me of their conversations in that tent, conversations about their families, life, the future. They spent ninety-six hours getting to know each other in a setting that forced the hand of authentic knowing.

"We made it to the summit; things were going well. Then, on the way down, the incident happened."

Another pause.

"Wanna hear something really weird?" he asked.

"Sure."

"We all had roles on the climb," he told me. "Mine was to be the first guy out on the ropes on descents, traverses, and ascents. I had done that every time. In fact I had been on that first rope at least fifty times so far on the climb." Pause. "There was only one time when I didn't go first . . . *that* time. The one time when it turned out to be a matter of life and death, my buddy went first."

We both pedaled for a while.

"Why? Why didn't I go first that time? Why am I still here? Why am I still alive?"

He took more heavy breaths, heavier than our efforts required.

He went on, processing his questions and thoughts in real time, "I don't really go to church much anymore. When I did, I was Lutheran. Well, I suppose I still am, I'm just not very religious."

I wondered where he was going with this. Then he said, "You want to be surprised again?" I didn't think he was looking for a verbal response. He continued.

"This is weird, but when my friend died—right after he died—I prayed for him and his family, and as I opened my eyes I saw the brightest white light I've ever seen in my life. It came right out of my friend and went straight up into the sky." We both put in ten pedal strokes. "You realize, don't you," he said, "that Lutherans don't see white lights when people die." I smiled. "Maybe Pentecostals do, but not Lutherans," he said.

Then he continued, "There's something going on here. This is going to change everything. Who is this God and what does he have for me?"

We had a great talk over the next few miles about his overwhelming sense that he has a purpose in life—that he's still here for a reason. I could hear a resolve in his voice, a commitment to searching answers to his "why" questions.

This guy, Mike, has a great journey ahead of him. We're getting together for lunch next week to talk some more. I can't wait.

We rode together for fifteen miles today. I thought it was going to be fifteen feet. I thought I was training for a bicycle race. God seemed to have me training for a race of much greater significance. I'm so glad I didn't blow past him. What would I have missed? What would Mike have missed? This story doesn't have an ending yet, but it almost never had a beginning. It was a split second away from never happening at all. These thoughts humble me.

He stopped at our house on the way back, and I gave him a copy of *Blue Collar God/White Collar God* (my first book) and asked him to read the Hip-Pocket God story. I got his number; he took mine. He left.

My head was buzzing so I decided to keep riding — get my interval workout in. Five miles into it I ran into another guy riding an old Bianchi bike, vintage. Never met him before. He told me he's trying to find the things that give him meaning in life. Who are these guys and where are they coming from today? He said he got some meaning from riding (I buy that) and gardening (that's a stretch). Then he turned and was gone. But I got his name and I'm going to Google him. Maybe we'll run into each other later this month. Wouldn't surprise me.

A block later I ran into Miles and Jennifer, a brother and sister out jogging. That's a surprise right there. Did you ever jog with your sister when you were in high school? Not me. I know their dad pretty well. We ride together. And for the past three years I led a small group for high schoolers. Miles attended on and off, so we know each other pretty well. He's also a musical prodigy, so we have that connection. (The musical part, not the prodigy part.)

We talked for a minute, then he said, "Let's get together before I go back to school. You know, talk about life, the future, you know." Cool. I hadn't known he wanted to talk to me about "life, the future, and you know." I need to call him to set that up.

I'm starting to realize that everything goes somewhere. Makes me wonder how many "somewheres" I've missed. They can be so subtle. I really want to miss fewer of them. I'm finding that they're so dang interesting. So fun.

So *surprising*.

DAY THREE: FLOATING

"I went to the theatre with the author of a successful play. He insisted on explaining everything. Told me what to watch, the details of direction, the errors of the property man, the foibles of the star. He anticipated all my surprises and ruined the evening."

"Never again!"

"And mark you, the greatest Author of all made no such mistake!"

Christopher Morley said that. Obviously the whole Surprise Me thing isn't original to me. Duh.

I was surprised when my niece, Vonda, e-mailed that quote to me. Surprised because she lives a thousand miles away, and I haven't spoken to her in a year. It turns out her mother (that would be my sister) told her about my little experiment and she decided to "half-heartedly take it on for herself." (Her words, not mine.) When she read that quote she thought I might be interested. Duh, again.

She fed me other things too. A quote from Ravi Zacharias, "Prayerlessness is the scavenger of wonder." I like that. And I know it's true because I've been there. And another quote from Ravi, "My deduction is that a praying Christian is carried by wonder; a prayerless person carries the wonder and will soon get exhausted by carrying the infinite." That got me thinking. And thinking often sends me into metaphorical land — the theater of rumination. Follow me there for a moment.

Imagine that we are hot-air balloons, and prayer is the hot air. What if the sky is where all the surprises hang out? Our prayers fill and give shape to our balloons, the containers of our souls, sending us straight into the clouds of surprise and wonder. We bump into them. They flow and drift by and through us. We can feel them, touch them. From our vantage point these surprises are our reality. It's exhilarating.

But when the prayers stop, we lose lift, we lose shape, we lose perspective, we lose the thrill of flying, we lose proximity to the sky-full of surprises because the gravity of prayerlessness has pulled us down. We can still see the surprises, but they're so far above us that they're barely discernible. They look suspiciously like circumstances. And we may even question if we actually saw them. Our balloons, our *lives* sag and lose shape.

When we stop praying, our lives get deflated.

I saw a hot-air balloon last night. It was shaped and painted like Mickey Mouse, ears and all. Walt Disney — now there was a guy who believed in wonder and surprise. He must have been a perpetual kid at heart. Kids seem to float more naturally. Maybe they're lighter spiritually, not carrying so much heavy baggage. They *believe* instinctively while we *question* dutifully.

If we truly believed like children, would we gravitate toward a more serious passion for prayer? Or if we formed a more passionate pattern of prayer, would we more willingly believe? (That chicken and egg thing always messed me up.)

Jesus loved kids and they loved him. He told us to be like them. Maybe that's part of what this experiment is about. Becoming more kid-like. Believing *just because.* I know some of you are a little uncomfortable with that last statement. It makes me 'squirm and twitch' a little too. But do you ever think that we adults, and I use that term loosely, test and question the living daylights out of everything to the point that we never allow ourselves to believe anything? Which is worse, misbelieving occasionally, or believing nothing at all?

Okay, roll credits on my metaphor and rumination. Time to head back out into reality. (Don't let the afternoon sun blind you as you exit the theater.)

I spent the biggest part of today helping my oldest daughter, Brianna, move into her first post-college apartment.

I was surprised by a couple of things. First, how Spartan it was. It ain't the Ritz. I'm not even sure if it's a HoJos. But Bri couldn't have been more excited. She talked a lot about decorating—*this will go here and that will go there.* "Pretty nice, don't you think, Dad?"

"*Mmmm.* Oh, yeah, it, uh . . . sure is . . . pretty nice."

Our house was never showcased on Robin Leach's *Lifestyles of the Rich and Famous,* or MTV's *Cribs,* but it's probably a few steps above Bri's current interpretation of "pretty nice." At least I think so. But Bri's eyes were twinkling as she gave me the 13.2-second tour of the tenement. There was a joy in her voice, in her stride, everything. There was float in her balloon. She was viewing her new digs contextually, not comparatively. She was happy about what it was, not disappointed about what it wasn't. I guess twinkle is in the eye of the beholder, and the weight of a particular surprise is relative to that twinkle.

The second surprise at the apartment was "The Unbearable Being of Lights-on." Bri seemed to be going for the "less is more" approach to lighting a room. She didn't want to leave any lights on, not even when we walked from one room to another. Taylor and I tested her, flipping lights on every chance we had. She followed us around and casually flipped them off. I finally called her on it.

"What's the deal with the lights?"

"Well, I don't have to pay for heating, but I do have to pay for electricity. So . . ."

Now, a little background info is appropriate here. This girl has never shown any serious tree-hugging or ozone-protecting tendencies. Until today, electricity was a limitless commodity that needed to be used in order to feel loved. Lights were left on to keep the rooms from getting lonely in Bri's absence. But the lights in her apartment seem to have different needs. They're surprisingly happier when turned off. And don't even mention air conditioning — it's on the endangered species list. All of a sudden, rationing is "in."

My youngest daughter, Taylor, came along to help with the move. She held the doors. She's fifteen, and she floats a *lot*. The ride home was fun because she was soaring. She had brought a little stash of CDs she'd burned (some of them legally) and was introducing me to some of the "newest bands that I needed to know about." She's got great taste in music. (Interpretation: we like a lot of the same stuff.)

When Tay was about six or seven I was doing the Christmas campaign for Target. I hired Amy Grant to sing the lead, and our little Taylor did a duet with Amy. Tay was so excited about this duet that her balloon must have been at about thirty-thousand feet. I had to give her oxygen. She still has the lyric sheet on her wall, signed by Amy.

Riding with her in the car and watching her feel the music — practically *become* the music — well, it was so cool. I'm not sure I'd call it a surprise, but there was joy and wonder in the moment.

The rest of the day was difficult for me. I struggled with one of the Miami/Latin sounding music spots I had to do for the Spirit FM package. I guess I just wasn't in the mood to merengue.

Now it's almost 1 a.m. This experiment is going to be difficult. If I can't find time until ten or eleven at night to start writing, I'm going to be one tired puppy in twenty-seven days. I am enjoying it though. I can see how this journaling thing could get addictive. It certainly helps to think through the details of the day — it gives perspective.

Maybe journaling is a form of prayer. When I write I can almost feel God whispering thoughts to me. And as I hunt and peck my thoughts back to him I think we're communicating in a keyboard-and-monitor-and-hard-drive-meets-high-flying-hot-air-balloon sort of way. I hope so, because I don't want my wonder to be scavenged. I don't want to miss the surprises because I'm flying too low to the ground.

It's been a long day and I'm starting to fade. Pretty soon, no amount of loft will keep me from doing a face-plant into my iMac.

See you tomorrow.

DAY FOUR: COW PIES

Today's first stop on the Surprise Me Express was an e-mail. The first publisher responded. That's fast! Same day. They said they loved the idea. They also said they don't want to taint the experiment so they suggested I finish the thirty-day deal and then talk.

Actually that was the second surprise. (Who can keep track?) The first came while reading Charlie Peacock's book *New Way to Be Human*. In his first chapter he quotes 1 Corinthians 2:9, "No eye has seen, no ear has heard, no mind has conceived what God has prepared for those who love him." I'd been looking for a verse that captures the essence of Surprise Me and there it was staring at me from another book. "No eye, no ear, and no mind" — I love that. Never seen, never heard, and never imagined. In other words, God is going to shock our socks off.

You would think people who believe this would be perpetually giddy, living as if it's Christmas Eve every day and God's just come back from shopping for us. What's under the tree today? Can't wait to see. Can't wait to wake up and open the gifts and *live*. Sadly, it seems that many Christians aren't smitten with this. I have to admit that I'm not there either much of the time.

Charlie wrote, "When I started hanging out with Christians, they seemed to be largely a people of dry, almost mathematical certainty." Ouch. I say we end that right here and now. *God, I want to unwrap all of the gifts you have for me today. Don't let me leave any of them under the tree.*

I just hung up the phone after talking to a member of my extended family. I woke up thinking about her today, so in an effort to not miss something, I called her. I'm glad I did. She's going through one of the hardest times of her life right now. I can't go into the details, but it's enough to say that when someone pops into your head, you need to call or e-mail them right away. It's spiritual "mojo." And when we act on that mojo, we get a gift — the dew that God dumps on us. The surprises.

Mary, my better two-thirds, is working again today so I'm off to lunch with my little Tator Tot (that would be Taylor — and she's gonna love that I just revealed this little nickname to the world). It will be just the two of us for lunch. And then I have a really important appointment for a haircut. Hope there aren't any surprises with the scissors.

Tay and I went to eat at a sidewalk café called Chez Foley. French. Tasty. Two of her friends work there and they spent a lot of time at our table. One of them just returned from France where she stood on the Champs Élysées and watched Lance Armstrong ride by to take his sixth consecutive Tour de France title. I'm jealous. If any of you out there are looking to really surprise me (*wink, wink*), an all expense-paid vacation to the Tour would take my breath away . . . but I won't hold it.

As I'm getting my hair cut (not at Chez Foley . . . I've moved on from there — stay with me people.) I notice that the snip-snip of the scissors is sounding very close, like *inside* my ear. I look up only to realize that it *is* coming from inside my ear. Nina is trimming ear hair. My ear hair. I'm not supposed to have ear hair till I'm old. Surprise?

Back home I pounded away at more music for this radio station. No big surprises there, although sometimes I'm still surprised how fun my job is. It's not easy, but it beats being on the Port-a-Potty pickup patrol. (Sorry. Don't mean to diss the Biff boys.)

I still love making music, but the ad biz has lost a bit of its fizz for me. I remember the day the carbonated world of TV commercials popped its last bubble. An ad agency called and asked me to write a jingle for a product called Inhibitor Bolus.

"Say what?" I had no clue what that was. (Be honest . . . did you? No? Well keep reading and I'll make you smarter than you wanna be. Trust me, you don't want to know this.)

They explained.

"Well, it's this big, honkin' pill that a farmer forces a cow to swallow. The pill meanders through the cows insides and when she, uh, deposits her pie in the pasture, well um, that freshly baked pie is laced with a chemical that inhibits the reproduction of flies."

Long pause.

I said, "Let me see if I have this straight. You want me to write a jingle for a product that kills flies in cow pies?"

"That's pretty much it."

It was at that very moment that I had one of the only epiphanies I've had in my life. I was raised in a predominantly German community and Germans don't have epiphanies, unless they've had too much stout with their kraut. Anyhow, the image that came to me was a vision of my future grandchildren standing in a cemetery looking at my tombstone. Interestingly, I could read my tombstone too, even though I was theoretically under it. It simply said,

"Here lies Terry Esau. He helped kill house flies in cow pies."

I got a deathly shiver. The cow pies were giving me goose bumps.

I hadn't really thought too much about my legacy before. I had a good career. Good money, good times, and I had promoted a lot of products that improved people's lives. It's good, I told myself.

As I hung up the phone I started thinking through the last decade of my music making. There was that Kitty Litter spot—good for cats and people. A few dozen herbicide and pesticide spots—good for crops, made farmers jobs easier, maybe not so good for the environment. Target—everybody loves Target. Well maybe not Wal-Mart, but they'll get over it. Golden Grahams—*Mmm.*

37

I went through a list of products and companies I had helped promote. From McDonald's to Shoney's, Harleys to Hondas, pickles to Pepsi . . . to the Mall of America. I noticed something when I looked over this list. Almost everything on the list "improved" people's lives, but nothing had the power to "change" them.

Not one single thing.

That started to bother me. A lot.

I know that focusing on this God I believe in can do me more good than cruising to the Mall of America on a Harley with a Pepsi in one hand and a pickle in the other. I know that "change" beats "improved." I'm beginning to understand that these stories I'm telling have a strange sort of power embedded in them I can't explain. I never once said that about one of my jingles.

I tell you this to say that "epiphanies" can mess with your head. In a good way. Mine prompted me to look for something different, something more to invest my life in, something life-changing. This Surprise Me deal is a stepchild of that epiphany, or at least a distant cousin. So, indirectly, Surprise Me was incubated in a nice, warm cow pie. A *fly-less cow pie*, mind you.

There's a lot more to my pre-Surprise Me journey I'd love to tell you, but maybe I'll save that for another day—one that's surprise-less. Will I have any of those?

I had a great ride this afternoon with three of my regular riding buddies. I love riding with these guys. Tom had a surprise going up a hill. His cable snapped so he was stuck with one gear for the rest of the ride. We all decided to put our bikes in the same gear and share Tom's pain. Well, until some young dude passed us. Then Gary, Bob, and I dropped a few gears faster than you can say "teenage testosterone still lives in middle-aged men" and we proceeded to hunt him down like an injured rabbit. Don't feel too bad for Tom. We *did* wait for him in the next town. Okay, okay . . . we were just trying to catch our breath.

I love speed. Let me restate that: I LOVE SPEED!

I registered no surprise at how much I love riding with my friends. I'm not sure I could buy therapy that restores me like riding does. And speaking of good therapy, tonight we went to a party with some old friends. Friends we haven't seen for a while. We grilled and ate outside and laughed so loud I thought the neighbors might call the cops.

Mary and I have been realizing something more and more lately. We are rich in friends. *Filthy stinking* rich. We know so many people who mean the world to us, and, by the way they treat us, I can tell they feel the same way too. There was no "dry, mathematical certainty" about this group tonight. I wonder if God was surprised? I hope he was listening in and thinking, "Now that's what I like to see — hugs, belly-laughs, authenticity, and a love of life."

Tomorrow should be fun. I'm meeting with one of my favorite nineteen-year-olds. This guy processes life like a Veg-o-matic, slicing and dicing away. He's got an insatiable curiosity that keeps him digging. He doesn't know exactly what he believes right now but is learning to enjoy this season of questioning. Questioning isn't a bad thing at all, when it comes to matters of faith. T. S. Eliot said, "Doubt and uncertainty are merely a variety of belief."

Sleep on that one. I think I will, too . . . right away . . . it's a quarter to one in the morning.

DAY FIVE: RULES OF PUNCTUATION

I got an e-mail from an author friend of mine this morning. Not sure what to make of it. After reading about my experiment she said, "Enjoy and endure the next 26 days. I am a little scared for you!!" Yes, she put two exclamation marks at the end. Authors usually don't mess with the rules of punctuation like that.

Is she telling me, "Be careful what you ask for. You just might get it"? Is walking through the door of Surprise like Red Riding Hood walking in on the wolf dressed as her grandmother?

A lot of people think that way—it's the "God's out to get me" syndrome.

I don't think that's what my author friend was saying. She has probably opened herself up to God and invited him to "have at her" for her own good and found that sometimes it's not all that pleasant. She's right. Maybe I should be scared. At least a little. Maybe I am. Just a little.

My nineteen-year-old friend Riggins and I found a table outside Starbucks and co-opted it for a couple of hours. It really was just a couple hours, but somewhere during our time together he turned twenty. His mom informed me later in the day that it was his birthday. He never even let on. I could have surprised *him*—a Vanilla Bean Frap with a birthday cherry on top.

We started out with small talk. He's heading off to college at UCLA. Yeah, I feel sorry for him too. I see surfing and babes in his future. Maybe a little studying, too. He was supposed to fill out a Roommate Checklist

Chart and send it in to the University. The Roommate Checklist Chart is this amazing document, devised by psychologists or wizards or monkeys, that helps school officials select just the right combination of students to share a room.

Yeah, right.

The Roommate Checklist Chart (let's just call it the RCC) features a bunch of those "choose one of these two options" pairings to help with the roommate matching. Partier vs. Studious. Night owl vs. Early bird. Smoker vs. Allergies. Sports vs. Chess club. God vs. Girls. (Okay, I made that last one up. God and girls aren't mutually exclusive — but the second one can certainly distract you from the first. Shoot, when you're nineteen — strike that, twenty — girls can distract you from just about anything. Make that everything.)

Riggins didn't fill out his RCC. He wanted to be surprised. His parents didn't think that was such a good idea. He liked the role chance might play in the roommate lottery; his parents wanted to rule out any possible hazards by filling out the RCC. I can see his parents' point — it's our role to protect. I can see his point, too — he wants to react to life as it happens. I don't know if one is wrong and the other right. It was an interesting discussion though.

He's got an interesting wrestling match going right now. He swallowed a view of God when he was young that's giving him spiritual indigestion. Now the question is what to do with this view of God. Does he throw it out? Does he remodel it? Does he find another God that goes down easier? Or does he just keep eating the bad chicken, because that's what good "bad-chicken-eaters" do — they just buck up and move on.

Maybe I'm nuts (we've pretty much established that, haven't we?), but I have this sneaking suspicion that this questioning mode he's in is exactly where God wants him. He's pressure-washing his faith and finding out what's under the religious film. He's testing and proving to himself that what he holds as truth really *is* truth — not just the hand-me-down beliefs of his parents or the pew-theology of his church or the bar-stool philosophy of his friends. He's de-botulizing his faith. There's bacteria in the baptismal, and he's the pool guy. Until you make your faith your own, you're just wearing somebody else's faith. Which, of course, may look good to "somebody else," but makes about as much sense as trying on shoes that are three sizes too small simply because someone else tried them on and they fit.

Why is it, by the way, that it's so important for us to look good? Who are we looking good for? And what constitutes looking good? Is my "good" the same as your "good"? And if not, whose good is the right good? And why is it that so often the brand of good we see as the accepted variety seems bad, or at least fake? Some "goodness" seems almost like a *portrayal* of goodness, not the real deal — bad posing as good.

Here's a surprise. I'm surprised that God doesn't flood this dump again. Rainbows = good! (You'll note I used just one exclamation mark. You won't find me messing with the rules of punctuation.)

Tay, Chelsea, and I went to lunch at Italiani's. Lauren was working and waited on us. We made sure she earned her 21 percent tip — yeah, I'm always going that extra 1 percent for my kids. She didn't have any sauce on her shirt yet, but I could sense the alfredo was planning a surprise attack.

Later, I took Tay and friends to a movie. I went to *The Bourne Supremacy* while they went to something else. (You can't be seen in a theater with your dad, you know — that's just wrong.) The movie was based on a Robert Ludlum book. I think I've read most of his books — each of them packed with intrigue, drama, espionage, and thrills. I especially liked his Bourne series, chock-full of surprises. Do you think that reading those books was part of my preparation for Surprise Me? Sometimes when I look back at my life I see things from decades ago that seem to have been a classroom prep course for what was yet to come.

My "then" was preparing me for my "now." I expect my "now" is preparing me for my "post-now." Of course since I don't yet know what my post-now will be, I can't really understand how my now is preparing me for it. And I don't know what parts of my now are the really important parts. Maybe they all are. Maybe the fact that I can't predict all that stuff should make me live totally in the moment of now so I don't miss the point of post-now.

(Go ahead and re-read that last paragraph. It's okay. It took me a while to compose it, so you're welcome to take the time necessary to understand it — if that's even possible.)

At the end of the day, Mary and I walked Bailey under a full moon. It was so bright there was a daylight quality to the evening. The shadows were vivid — so well-defined that every once in a while Bailey jumped at the sight of our shadows dancing on the far side of the ditch. She used to bark at them when she was a puppy, but I think she's finally figured out that shadows don't bite.

Bailey's unfounded fear reminds me of my author friend's e-mail. Should I fear the invitation of surprise? Will I find myself jumping at shadows? Will any of the surprises nip at my heels? I wonder.

This is the second full moon of the month. You know when people say "once in a blue moon"? Well this is it — when everything lands just right so you get two full moons in one month. It only happens once every three years. It seems fitting that something rare and beautiful would add another exclamation mark to my day.

God can mess with the rules of punctuation all he wants.

DAY SIX: AGENDA SABOTEURS

It's 1 p.m. and I'm a bit frustrated. Tomorrow we leave for New York on a quick two-day getaway with our girls. I'm trying to book a hotel online. So far the surprises have been of the sticker-shock variety. Do you realize that a twelve-year-old is considered an adult when booking a room? And it's fifty bucks extra, per night, for that "adult." Taylor is 15, well 16 in a week. Don't they know that she's my baby? My baby can't be an adult, that would make me . . . never mind.

So I've been dancing with Expedia.com, Priceline.com, and Hotels.com all morning. They're all stepping on my toes. Dotcoms are lousy dancers! You do the lengthy routine, then they tell you, sorry that's too many "adults" in one room. One said, "We could give you a two-bedroom suite for all the money you have in your retirement plan—plus, we'll have to conscript that fifteen-year-old daughter to a lifetime of service as a maid in order to cover the cost of the free concierge service." I told them I couldn't consign her to this life of servitude because, EVIDENTLY, she's an adult now, and I no longer have that authority.

After much frustration, I found a hotel that offers everything I need—except that it's available for only one of the two nights. So I started over. Found another one. I decided to call them directly to see if I could get a better rate over the phone. Nope. Apparently, talking to Real Live People costs an extra $75 per night. Did someone put helium in the commission balloon? When I went back to the website, I found that the price was now $100 more per night. What?!? I was only gone three minutes! It's a freakin' conspiracy! Did somebody slap a "Take-me-to-the cleaners" note on my back?

I finally booked a room. It'll be nice. It better be! (I wonder if pawn shops take carbon fiber bikes with a second mortgage on them?)

I realized something through this process today. I hate it when my agenda is held hostage by an activity I deem to be of less value. Do you know what I'm talking about? There are a lot of, um, let's call them "tasks" that rob time from my day. These agenda saboteurs threaten the sanctity of my carefully planned life. They are The Things I Don't Think I Should Have to Do.

I have my own hierarchical view of the activities that make up my existence. I'm not sure how I constructed the schematics of this flowchart, but it makes sense to me. Maybe my beef with tasks is misplaced. Maybe the tasks are just benign blips that only get their charted position based on their relationship to me. If I think highly of myself, then the tasks are "below" me. If I don't think so highly of myself, then the tasks fit perfectly within the realm of my duties.

But . . . .

I'm a little frustrated right now, maybe even a little angry because we're booked on the 9:30 a.m. flight tomorrow. You may recall I've been talking about racing in the State Championship Criterium bike race this weekend. Last year I finished third in that race, and I've relived the last hundred meters in my mind a couple of times—give or take several hundred. I know I can do better. I think I can. Well, there is an outside chance I could. The race starts at 10:30 a.m. tomorrow. But the flight that worked out the best for all of us leaves at 9:30. Do you see the scheduling problem? What do I do with that?

It complicates things for the family if I fly out separately. They're not comfortable navigating the Big Apple without me. I admit I have a little anger about that too. Dependency has always seemed like a weakness to me. I want my wife and daughters to look me in the eye and say, "No problem, we can handle this on our own. We are capable!" Can you hear strains of "I am woman, hear me roar" in the background?

I wasn't crazy about taking this trip in the first place. I'm swamped. My life is like the plate of an eighteen-year-old football lineman at the Old Country Buffet. (Do they know that they can go back to the food line as many times as they want?)

You're probably noticing that I have some "self" issues. I don't want my world to be dominated. I don't want to be leaned on when I'm not in the supporting mood. I don't want my agenda altered. I don't want to have my day defined by "tasks." And I don't want to be at the mercy of other people.

Whoa, that's a lot of "I"s, and they're staring back at me. Telling me with their Clint Eastwood gaze that I may just have a problem with control. I'll grant that. But if that's my MO, then maybe I need to rethink the basic premise of this experiment. If maintaining autonomy and control is what I really want, then praying "Surprise Me" every day is not a very bright idea, now is it? By saying those words to God I'm placing my life at the mercy of someone other than me. It's an invitation for God to alter my agenda. It's a flowchart without "Terry" at the top of the page. It means taking smaller portions in the buffet line and leaving room for God and others to put something on my plate.

Maybe this is what my author friend was talking about when she said, "I'm a little scared for you."

Yet still my wrestling continues. What if God *wants* me to send my family off on their own? What if he wants to stretch them — to give them an opportunity to grow, to build self-confidence? It's possible, right? Am I just rationalizing? Trying to get what I want?

It may sound like I'm frustrated by all of this thinking. But really, I enjoy it. It's how I make sense of things. I find satisfaction in this psychological and spiritual wrestling. Maybe I should have been a shrink. (Although instead of showing people ink blotches I would have played them funk grooves and asked them what they heard in-between the beats.)

It's 10:30 p.m. now. The decision has been made about tomorrow. I will go to the airport with the fam. I feel good about the decision. Besides, now I can live another year in "if-land" — the place where all cyclists go when circumstances prevent them from competing in a race that surely would have landed them on a Wheaties box. In if-land, I would have taken first or second place this year. I may need to spend more time in if-land now that I'm cresting the "hill." (You know, the one you go "over" at a certain age.) My accomplishments in if-land would likely be far superior to those in reality-land.

Maybe this if-land concept can shed some light on the idea of faith.

In bike racing, if I never actually engage in the competition, but only theorize about it, my reality of the experience will only ever be theoretical. I will only be able to measure the success of my skills *theoretically*. My passion for racing will only be what I can imagine.

In our faith, if we never actually compete for our beliefs, *wrestle* with them, then we will never be able to touch them, feel them, hold them in our hands, or wear them around our necks. Our faith will never feel the road because we won't take it for a test drive.

While Mary and I walked Bailey this evening, an incredible lightning storm was surprising the sky. For a brief moment, we wondered if the surprise of the day might feature a megawatt shocker. It would sure make that e-mail I received earlier — "I am a little scared for you" — look like brilliant foreshadowing. It would also have made a great entry in this book — but then again, it would have made the book a whole lot shorter, too.

47

We made it through unscorched. There was no killer jolt tonight — no million-volt message telling me I should stop all this psycho-spiritual wrestling. Evidently there's no "Zap Me Now" sign on my back.

Maybe *that's* the surprise.

DAY SEVEN: TAXI DRIVER

I'm in seat 5B, looking down from 30,000 feet, and we're halfway to New York. I wonder how the State Championship race is going? (Let it go, Terry.) I just tossed out another "Surprise Me, God" prayer, adding to the one I said as I was walking Bailey this morning. Maybe from five miles up, the signal will come through a little more clearly.

Even though it's just day seven, I've noticed something interesting about this Surprise Me experiment: Virtually all of my "surprises" so far fall in one of two categories — people and God. They've come from and through relationships with old friends, new friends, people I run into on bicycle rides and at coffee shops. And I seem to run into that God guy almost everywhere, or maybe he runs into me (with one of us invisible, it's difficult to tell who ran into whom).

What I'm saying is, surprises seem to be largely a product of our contact with people and God. Inanimate objects, not so much. My toaster has never really shocked me, and I don't suppose I've surprised it too much either. New York — now this is a place with plenty of opportunity to be up close and personal with people. All kinds of people. All kinds of wall-to-wall people. I'm looking forward to the citified surprises.

I didn't have to wait long.

Our taxi ride from the airport to our hotel had almost enough breath-grabbers for the whole day. Our driver was on a mission to show all other motorists that the road — that the whole city — was his turf. "Everybody else, back off!" We played chicken with a lot of cars and trucks and taxis. One guy wouldn't back down so we sideswiped him, collecting a three-foot scratch-and-dent scar as a reminder of our vehicular victory. "We showed him. Didn't we?" Now, if this had happened back home in Minnesota, well, it would have been, "Uff da, did I do dat den der? I'm awful sorry. I was yust tinking about dis beautiful weather and wasn't paying no never-mind to my driving and . . ."

But not in New York. Neither our driver nor the other cabby did anything about the incident. Our driver didn't even react to the metallic scrunch, his face did and said nothing. He simply bottled it.

By the time we got to our hotel, I think his bottle needed to let off some steam. The bell captain asked him to turn off his car while we unloaded. He refused. They had some choice words for each other—and when I say "choice" I don't mean "Uff da, darn it!" The bell captain reached inside the taxi to turn it off and our cabby yelled, "Don't touch my car!" More "Uff da"-ish words. The bell captain won and our cabby killed the engine (though I think he would rather have killed the bell captain). Our driver, who thought he ruled the road, was now down 2-0. I wonder how the rest of his day went?

Boisterous banter is a staple of New York. It's a taboo in Minnesota. I think I should live in Ohio.

The first thing we did when we got to our room was turn on the TV. Habit. News flash: Terror alert goes to orange for NY city. The financial district had been targeted, including the Stock Exchange Building and the CitiBank building. Our hotel was one block away from Citibank. The reporter said there was "extremely credible" information that an attack on those buildings was likely. Welcome to the pressure cooker.

Later we walked by the building. (Probably not the smartest thing we ever did.) There were barricades everywhere. I carelessly spoke out loud a thought that popped into my head, "Wow. This would make the Surprise Me thing even more interesting." The family didn't think it was funny.

A sandwich—that's what we needed to forget about the danger. We found a funky little New York deli and ordered the "Bin-Laden-B-Gone" entree. Halfway through our paninis we had all but forgotten about the terrorists. We were sitting at a bar, looking out the front window onto the sidewalk. Tay felt a little uncomfortable staring out at people. She's so "Minnesota nice." The New Yorkers weren't even aware that we were staring.

After lunch we walked to Times Square and stood in a line to get discounted tickets for a Broadway show. On the way there we had our first taste of street-corner religion and ministers who have mastered the art of abrasive, in-your-face evangelism. One guy was yelling, "God loves everybody." Good. "God loves sinners." Good. "God even loves the sin." Huh? Welcome to the Theological Seminary of Times Square, Rationalization Department.

Later that night we went to see *Little Shop of Horrors*. It has an interesting plot. A humble, young botanist named Seymour creates a new breed of plant life and names his plant Audrey II, after his love interest, Audrey, who works with him in the flower shop. People start coming from far and wide to see Audrey II. Everything is going great until one day Seymour notices that the plant is dying. He doesn't know how to help Audrey II until he discovers, quite by accident, that his plant needs blood to live. Seymour then gives his own blood to nourish Audrey II and keep it alive.

Is this plotline starting to sound familiar?

After a while Seymour didn't have enough blood of his own. Audrey II was growing rapidly, and she had quite the appetite. He told the plant, "I can't give any more of my blood without actually dying myself." The plant just smacked its petals as if to say, *Mmmm*, do what you gotta do, baby."

51

Seymour's love for Audrey II gave him no choice. He put his arms out and dove willingly, headfirst to his death. It was a strange moment in the play. I could tell some people felt uncomfortable, like "couldn't the plot have gone somewhere else? Couldn't the writer come up with another solution for this predicament? If Seymour could create this species from nothing, you'd think he'd be able to come up with a less painful remedy than his own personal sacrifice."

Evidently not.

Still sound familiar to you? The parallels sort of fall apart after that, but the theme of sacrifice in Little Shop is surprisingly similar to what you'll find in the Bible—what a lover of green our God must be.

I think I've Miracle-Gro-ed this story about as far as possible.

After the show, we walked back to our hotel. There were a few dark streets with that typical New York smelly steam rising from the manholes. It was a bit eerie and my girls seemed to hug my shadow. It felt kind of good to know that they look to me for protection. I was glad, however, that I didn't have to "attempt" to provide it.

Today was a fun day. When we get away together, we're pulled out of our routines and tend to talk and interact differently. We're more relaxed. A lot of laughing and living took place today. I plopped into bed a happy camper—in spite of the fact that I missed my race.

Come to think of it, I did win the Airport to Hotel Taxi Criterium. That ought to count for something.

DAY EIGHT: LESSONS FROM PAM

It's Monday morning, and we're two blocks away from Rockefeller Plaza and the NBC Studios, which just so happens to be where the *Today Show* is shot. Every morning. *Right about this time.*

Mary ejects herself from the mattress.

"*Ahhh!* Let's go, outta bed you lazy bums!" She's on a mission.

Mary has a thing for Katie Couric. Don't get me wrong; Mary's plenty straight, but sometimes I wonder what my life would be like if I could interview like Katie or if I had a dimpled grin like Katie's. Maybe Mary would love me a bit more. We could be "girlfriends." Me, Mary, Katie, and Oprah. Swell.

Well, that's just not gonna happen.

Just the same, we went to watch the live taping of the *Today Show*. We stood elbow to elbow and sternum to scapula with hundreds of other birders straining for a glimpse of the rare Matt and Katie varieties only to find out that our little feathered friend was on vacation for the week. Must be migrating season. How could she do this to us? Didn't she know we were coming?

We stayed and watched for a while till we got hungry. Food wins over most things in our family. Glad we can agree on that.

After the ham and cheese croissants, we hopped a cab for Ground Zero. I expected it to have more of an emotional impact on me than it did. Everything was cleaned up so nice and tidy that it was almost hard to imagine what really happened there.

But as I looked at the hole that had once cradled the great Twin Towers, I thought about the atrocities that have been done in the name of God. Crusades, wars, jihads, "cleansings," massacres, punch parties, hooded white robes, and swastikas. God must look down on all this and go, "Hey, leave me out of that. Don't drag my holy name in to validate your hateful agendas. I liked those towers just as they were—with people inside them. I'm the love guy, remember? Hate's not really my thing."

Then it was over to Soho and purse shopping—because a guy like me can't have too many purses. Okay, I was basically the ATM machine for the day. My daughters would slide a purse over their shoulder, look at me and ask, "What do you think, Dad?" To which I have no good answer, except maybe, "Nice. Kinda reminds me of the other three black ones you have at home." But I don't say that because—well, actually I do say that sometimes. And sometimes it works and we walk out leaving that to-die-for bag for some other lucky shopper. Sometimes we walk out with it because we can't "need" it.

In all fairness, I buy some things that I'm sure my girls look at and go, "What? You paid how much for that?" They just don't understand that a carbon seat-post for my bike is a necessity. It's "to-die-for."

So, we shopped.

Later we hit the Tavern on the Green for dinner. Pretty cool setting, but it was nasty-expensive on the Esau ATM account. Mary and I decided to share a meal. They charged us $10 extra to split a steak. I should have just pilfered an extra fork and nibbled when our server was away on business. My girls say I'm cheap—like it's a *bad* thing.

After dinner we walked in Central Park. Hundreds of cyclists and joggers were going in the same circles they go in every day. I guess if you wanted to run around city blocks, you could run in squares, but in Central Park, it's circles. Here in the city, people live in boxes, stand in lines, walk in squares, and run in circles. Manhattan is geometric. It has logic and form. Structurally predictable, it makes sense.

My life isn't like Manhattan. It's not all circles and squares. It's got triangles and trapezoids and a bunch of other undecipherable 'zoids. Just when you think you're running in a circle, bam, the path ends and you're hexagoning. It's a maze of twists and turns. It rarely goes where you think it's going, and the path is seldom direct.

Life is asymmetric. It's unpredictable. Maybe that's why I like this Surprise Me experiment. It helps me to celebrate the unpredictability. It's teaching me to enjoy what I don't yet know, and to relish living in the middle of unfinished-ness. It's learning to love the shape of the day, the "'zoid du jour."

Just outside Central Park is a Kinkos, so we bopped in and checked our e-mail. Another publisher responded to the Surprise Me thing with interest. He said, "Oh. A thirty-day experiment, huh? People love books with numbers in the title. 40-This or 7-That. It's all good." Anyhow, they want to talk some more about it.

I wonder if they'll change their mind when they see this chapter where I describe how Pamela Anderson taught my family some spiritual insights.

Let me explain. No really, there's a good explanation.

The Letterman Show tapes at 5 p.m. We walked over to the Ed Sullivan Theater. We didn't have tickets and knew we weren't going to get any. They're spoken for long in advance, and I rarely "speak" for anything in advance. I'm spontaneously disorganized, always have been.

So we're hanging out outside the theater. First we go over to Rupert's Hello Deli, and there he was, as shy and unassuming as he is on the show. We got our picture taken with him, and I bought lemonade from his wife. They thanked me.

Then we found out that this evening's show was planning a watermelon drop from a window about four feet off the ground. They've dropped everything from computers to bowling balls to cakes from eight stories up, but tonight they wanted to see what gravity would do to a watermelon from the frightening altitude of four feet.

I was an eyewitness, and I can tell you it was a non-event. It split, but it didn't splatter. If you're going to toss fruit from a window, you want to see some splatter, some collateral damage. From four feet, nothing.

As I was preparing to witness this non-event, I left the safe haven of the two hundred or so Letterman audience rejects and casually wandered across the street to get a bird's-eye view. My wife gave me one of those terse whispers I've heard so many times, "Pssst, Terry, get back here! You're not allowed on that side of the street."

I gave her the look she's seen many times before that says, "Work with me here—play dumb like me." She allowed me to play dumb solo. This, too, is a pattern we've rehearsed to perfection over the years. So I walked across the street to a cordoned-off area that was home to a bunch of photographers with some serious equipment. I made some small talk with them and found out they were all there to snap photos of Pamela Anderson as she exited the theater and hopped into her limo. They weren't there for the watermelon. They were from the *Enquirer*, the *Globe*, the *Star*, and any and all other tabloids needing a photo that would help convince lonely men loitering around convenience stores to drop a buck on a Pamela sighting.

Now, the interesting thing about all this had almost nothing to do with Pam. (Mary called her that while we were waiting. It made me wonder if she knew her in a more personal way than I did, like they were tight or something. I'm going to call her Pam too now.) The interesting thing for me was watching this scene play out and observing the diverse characters in the play.

First, there were the casual passersby. These were the people who happened onto the scene and wondered what was going on. I could tell most of them didn't really have any emotional investment in Pam, but they figured as long as they were here at this time and place, they might as well stick it out and see what all the fuss was about.

Then there was the press. I'm hanging out with these guys and they didn't give a "you know what" about Pam. They were assigned to get some pics of the princess. They had a job to do. That's it. They didn't particularly want to be there. Several of them told me as much. One was frustrated and angry because he wanted to be with his family tonight, not stuck feeding the appetite of an attention-starved starlet and her malnourished fans.

Two girls who were part of the former group walked by "us" professional photographers and dryly threw out a question.

"What's all the fuss about? Is Jesus Christ on the show tonight?"

Without missing a beat, one of the photographers sarcastically threw an answer back at her, "No. Someone even better . . . Pamela Anderson!"

That leads me to the third group of players in our cast. The psycho, sex-starved, blonde-stalking nut cases. Sorry, that was a little harsh. But not by much. This group pushed and shoved their way to the front. Security had to barricade them away. Guards protected the limo to keep the fan-addicts from climbing in.

This group came with a whole array of paraphernalia. Many had old issues of Playboy in which Pam had posed. Some had blown-up photos of her affixed to a hardboard, complete with a felt-tipped pen so they could thrust it at her quickly in an attempt to get her priceless autograph. Some wore *Barb Wire* T-shirts — I think that was a movie she starred in. Some carried bouquets of flowers. Some came with nothing to offer but a bad case of bug eyes and chin drool.

Oh, and there was one little old lady. I mean, she had to be eighty-five if she was a day. I have no idea what her deal was, but she wasn't intimidated one bit by the drool or the daisies. Her elbows protected her space as effectively as anyone in the pack.

All of a sudden the press crew sprang to their feet and elbow-wrestled for position along the front of the barricade. The studio door opened and the drool-crew started screaming and waving their pictures and magazines toward the opening.

Out stepped a woman, but not THE woman. It was Pam's personal assistant. There was an audible sound of disappointment, "Ohhh." Everybody turned away. It made me wonder how she felt.

Pam = screams!

Pam's personal assistant = groans.

The excitement ebbed. Five more minutes. The press was seated again. Droolers, still front and center.

Finally the door opened and out stepped Pam. The three distinct groups saw her simultaneously, but very differently. This is how I'm guessing they saw her.

The passersby group saw tonight's guest of the Letterman show heading to her limo.

The press saw a paycheck.

The drool-crew saw Jesus Christ — in a green satin dress. They saw their savior, someone who could love them and make them feel loved. Someone who could give meaning to their lives, purpose to their existence. Someone for whom they would have, and probably did, walked miles just to touch the hem of her garment. Someone who simply by being with them would, by association, make them somebody.

As I watched all this go down, I was torn — it was so ridiculous it was funny, and yet it was so sad.

Pam grabbed someone's marker and flailed it in the general direction of the magazines and pictures. The group stretched their objects out to her hoping that they would by chance make contact on some point of the arc. She was looking away as she swung the pen back and forth. One thing I'll guarantee you, there were no legible autographs delivered today. The security pushed them back. The press yelled and screamed, trying to get her to cast a glance their way so they could get a paycheck.

Pam just dove for the cover of her car. The door slammed and . . .

. . . the passersby gawked, thinking, "Hmm, that was an interesting diversion in our day."

. . . the press screamed, "Crucify her! Crucify her!" Well, not literally. But when she never cast a glance their way, they felt the paycheck slip through their hands. When the limo door slammed, the cash register closed. "Show us some cleavage and a smile, you &*#$@!" they yelled.

. . . and the Droolers yelled, "Don't leave us, Jesus. We need you. Who are we without you? We can't live without you. If you would just love us, maybe, just maybe we would be somebody." Well they didn't really say those words either, but I swear I heard them just as plain as day.

Sadly, for everyone's sake — especially her own — Pam came back out. Evidently there's no limelight in limos. She put on a coy smile and soireéd out of the limo, twirling in her green chiffon dress. She posed and pouted her lips toward the motorized cameras that flashed like a fireworks finale on the fourth. It seems she needed their attention just as badly as they needed hers. Droolers and starlets are stuck in codependency cycles that cannibalize each other.

I couldn't help but think what a sad picture of the human condition this was. We want to be loved so badly, but we're so bad at knowing where and how to find it. God must be saying, "What do I have to do . . . that I haven't already done?"

As we walked through Times Square I asked my family for their impressions of the Pam scene. They thought it was pretty sad, too. Taylor observed that it must be awful to be a star, having weirdoes do that to you every time you tried to go grocery shopping, or go out for dinner, or anything.

She's right. That would be awful. And yet Pamela willingly got back out of the limo. Inside the limo, something was still missing, the something that could make her okay with who she is. So she got back out to continue looking for it.

Maybe that's the positive message here. We're all looking for something, and as long as we keep getting out of the limo, keep looking, there's a chance we'll find it. I think God created that emptiness so we would keep searching for the "significant something — or someone" to fill it.

Walking down the sidewalks of Manhattan, I looked at my girls and thought, "What's with the obsession with Pam? My daughters were there too, they're every bit as pretty." I told my girls that, and they didn't say much.

Maybe they were still processing the spiritual lessons of "Pam's Search for Meaning." Who knew celebrity sightings could be sermons?

Surprise.

DAY NINE: THE PURSE SKIRMISH

It's Tuesday. We head back home to Minneapolis this afternoon to a world I understand much better. At least I'm more accustomed to it. I think the Scandinavians sculpted the Midwestern culture out of logic, while the Italians had a bigger, gesticulating hand in chiseling this East Coast culture out of "What-a-ya-lookin-at-me-dat-way-fo?" And who knew car horns were a complete and exhaustive language?

Still, I'm really going to miss the lunacy of New York. I think the Big Apple was built for surprises. It's as if they have a daily SQ—Surprise Quota. That could become the city's slogan: "If you don't get one surprise per hour, somebody ain't doin' their job!" Maybe I should have spent all thirty days of this experiment in New York.

When the alarm went off this morning, Mary rolled over and said, "Well, you know, Katie Couric isn't there anyhow."

Hand—snooze button.

Later, after the requisite time for beauty sleep (not that any of us need it—well, except for me), we wandered the streets looking for a breakfast place we could all agree on. Hunger pangs and the omnipresence of Starbucks won out over unanimity. They had pastries and we had hunger. It was a good enough match.

As we wandered the city later in the day, we came across more street corner screamers holding Bibles. What's that all about? Why are so many "unique" people ranting about who-knows-what and threatening to slice and dice passersby with their Bibles? None of them were waving Pamela—excuse me—*Pam* Anderson's new book. None were waving

Bill Clinton's biography. It's always the Bible—God's biography.

We also noted that there is a lot of cursing tossed around the streets of New York. Some of it's pretty creative, more so than we might hear in Minneapolis. But most is pretty predictable. You've got your basic "God This" and "God That," and your more personal "Jesus H This" and "Jesus F That." (Who knew Jesus had so many middle names? It makes me wonder if Jesus is more popular with crazies and cursers than he is with us "regular" folk? And does that say more about us than it does about them?)

Incidentally, I've never heard anyone yell "Bill-*Freaking*-Clinton" or "Pamela *H* Anderson" after hitting his or her thumb with a hammer. For that matter, I've never heard anyone put an "H" after Allah or Vishnu either. It seems Judeo-Christian icons win the "Most Popular Pronouns for Use in Savvy Swearing" crown. I wonder why that is?

The girls saw and heard a variety of vulgarities today. I guess I have to live with that. I can't shelter them much longer anyhow—those days are over. This is the world we live in, and we need to live *in* it, not separated from it. Seems to me that's what Jesus did.

I bet Jesus would have loved New York. Perhaps when he and his Trinitarian pals were planning out history, Jesus lobbied to come to New York City in AD 2004 instead of Bethlehem right between BC and AD. What's Bethlehem got that New York hasn't got?

One thing's for sure, if Jesus had come to New York in 2004, he would most likely have been viewed as a crazy. Not because he would threaten bodily harm while swinging a Bible as a sword, but because he just wouldn't fit in. He would love people on the street, he would approach them, talk to them, touch them, befriend them, help them, sacrifice his comfort for theirs, and did I mention love them? He wouldn't look down his nose at the crazies and cursers like we do, but instead, might be disgusted—or at least saddened by us "normal" people. Us normal people who hang onto apathy, selfishness, certainty, self-right-ness, judgmentalism, and holier-than-thou-ness as tightly as one of those flailing Bibles. He might even send a little money-changer-ish wrath our way.

But just like 2,000 years ago, even disgust or sadness wouldn't diminish his love. He would have loved the cursers and the crazies. He would have loved the drool-crew from last night. He would have loved Pam Anderson. He would have loved her limo driver and her personal assistant.

If he had been here, he might have been one of the photographers, taking her picture, not for a paycheck, but just because he loved her. He might have been one of the rabid fans, but without the destructive motives and codependent insecurities — and without the Playboy centerfold. He might have been one of the passersby and just given a "thumbs-up" to her.

He might have even been me.

Wait a minute . . . he was me, or maybe I was him, or at least I had the opportunity to be him in that situation. I'm a follower of Christ so I get to be his twenty-first-century stand-in; I get to love people for him, like him, wherever I go. Ooh, there's a surprise I didn't see coming. Jesus could have come in 2004 and been at that Letterman fiasco in person, but he didn't, instead . . . he had *me* there. If my mission is to be Christlike to people in all situations, then I had an opportunity — maybe an obligation, to do what he would have done were he there in person.

So, what would he have done if he had been me last night?

Maybe Jesus wouldn't have been quite so intent on documenting the event with a camera. Maybe he wouldn't have felt quite so good about himself for psychoanalyzing the players in the drama. Maybe he would have spent more energy figuring out how to help them than simply to understand them. He would have already known their motives, so his next step would have been to heal their hurt, their hearts.

When I think about it, the one thing both Pam and the Droolers seemed to lack was the assurance that they were loved, simply and purely. How would he have communicated that to them? How could I have done that?

Should I have yelled, "Pam—Pamela, God loves you just the way you are." They would have thought I was crazy; I wonder what she would have done if I had yelled that?

I honestly don't know what I should have done. Maybe telling you all about this is part of what I was supposed to do. So when you run into a situation like this (and what are the odds of that?) you might think twice about your role, your reactions. Maybe you will look for ways to communicate love instead of judgment. If that's the result, then the story of Pam and the Droolers will have had a good ending.

(Pam and the Droolers—sounds like the name of a seventies rock band, doesn't it? I can see their worldwide tour now: The Droolapalooza Tour.)

We had an early flight, so New York didn't get much of us today, or maybe we didn't get much of it. The ride back to LaGuardia was infinitely saner than the ride from it. Tony Soprano wasn't our driver this time. Lady Liberty threw us a kiss as our plane banked to the west.

Back on the ground in Minne-apple-es, we tossed our carry-ons into the back of the Rover and headed off to meet Bri and Brian for dinner. (Brian is Bri's boyfriend . . . conveniently named, don't you think? Kismet?) We went to Friday's, and Mary and I split a meal because we were already full from the delicious airline cuisine. Incidentally, there was no $10 surcharge for the split.

We sat, ate, laughed, and told stories of the last few days. Oh, and we gave Bri the purse we bought for her on Canal Street.

"Is this really a Louis Vuitton?" she asked.

"Oh yeah," I said, "I dropped some big bills on that baby." She believed me for about a negative two seconds. But then we had to tell her the whole story of . . .

THE PURSE SKIRMISH — FINDING LOUIS

The cab dropped us at Canal Street because our sources told us this was the Mecca of knock-off designer purses. Can you feel the excitement? I'm all goosebumply. We rambled from one hole-in-the-wall shop to the next looking for a Louis that looked real. Taylor, the bravest of our handbag hunters, would ask, "Do you have any Louis'?"

The clerk would look around, and then dig into an apparently random purse dangling from a hook on the wall and pull out a little photo album with pictures of the Vuittons they had tucked away in the back room. Tay would point to one and say, "Do you have that one?" The clerk would discreetly nod and say, "I'll be right back."

She would disappear through a poorly disguised trap door on the back wall and show up a few minutes later with a knock-off purse that invariably was not the one that Taylor had pointed to.

This went on for a while . . . a stinking long while, if you ask me. We were in a dozen shops and some shop owners seemed concerned about that, while others seemed oblivious to them. The cops obviously know that all these stores are selling knock offs and yet they weren't exactly arresting anyone.

Finally, after we were all getting a little tired of this game, a lady came up to us on the street and said, "You want Louis Vuitton? I have many. Come look."

She had a walkie-talkie and handed us off to another woman who shuttled us down an alley, in a side door, up some rickety stairs, down a hall, then handed us off to another walkie-talkied lady who punched a code into a door lock. We walked inside and she locked the door behind us. This was getting fun. There was a little of that S & T factor, the Squirm and Twitch, to let us know we were onto something interesting. It was starting to feel like a Bond movie and I was 007 himself. (Of course I'm married, and I'm, uh, well, purse shopping with my daughters . . . but other than that, it was exactly like a Bond movie.)

We went through another set of doors into . . . the Holy of Holies. There, in all its gorgeous glittering glory, was a treasure trove of Louis Vuittons—enough to schlepp around a warehouse full of Clinique. This was the Holy Grail of handbag collections. The Hope Diamond of satchel sanctuaries. This was Al Capone's vault how Geraldo had imagined it.

I holstered my 45 and . . . wait, sorry, I got carried away there.

Mary, Tay, and Lauren got a premature glimpse of heaven. The streets weren't gold, but the walls were covered in it. Talk about kids in a candy store. I could almost see the enamel being eaten away on my credit card.

We did some dealing. Ended up with a gaggle of purses—purses for friends, relatives, and pets. Okay, not pets, but it was a lot of purses. We reversed our entry procedure and were redeposited in the alley with our bags filled with bags.

We swaggered down Canal Street with our booty. I leaned over and kissed my wife, full on the lips, in a very Bond-esque manner as if to say, "Not only did I get the woman, but I got the purses . . . and, of course, restored world peace."

I'm not sure if Bri and Brian bought the whole story, but it's true. Guys don't make up stories about purse shopping. And I've got to admit, if shopping for handbags was always that much fun, I'd volunteer to go along a little more often.

We got home in time to take Bailey for a walk and check out the stars over Minneapolis. I'm sure New York is still wide-awake, but I'm putting that Apple to sleep. She was a fun date for a couple of days and she taught me some things I wasn't expecting. But now I'm home. I love it here. The surprises will be different than in New York. But they'll be there.

I look forward to being shaken by them. (Not stirred.)

(Cue James Bond theme song.)

DAY TEN:
A CHRISTMAS STORY

Never thought I'd say this, but I asked God to surprise me by making my life as interesting as purse shopping. Don't tell anyone I said that, okay?

It's true, my life and this Surprise Me experiment is a bit like the Purse Skirmish — you go down an alley, up some rickety stairs, through hallways and locked doors, handed from one walkie-talkie-toting escort to the next, never quite sure where you're headed, but hoping that eventually you'll find what you're looking for.

Life is just a quest for the right purse.

Today, as I was thinking about our Canal Street experience, it occurred to me that our steps down the alley, up the stairs, and through hallways and locked doors were all being directed by someone on the other end of a walkie-talkie. But who? Who was calling the shots in the search for the holy handbag?

Obviously it was someone who knew where the purses were. Had it been the mob-boss of the flip-flop trade directing us, we would have ended up in the flip-flop showroom. We might have said, "Hmmm, nice flip-flops sir, but I kind of had a hankering for purses today, not flip-flops." If you've got the wrong guy on the walkie-talkie, you might never get where you want to go.

I like the idea of our lives having a little double-oh-seven mystery to them, but it seems important that we know what and how and who is directing it. You don't want an idiot running a spy operation, and you certainly don't want a moron orchestrating your life.

From all indications, God isn't a moron. The universe is fairly well put together. My guess is he knows where the purses are. So if he says, "Take a right at the next stairway and then left down the hall," I probably ought to take that suggestion seriously. If heaven is what you're shopping for, it follows that the guy you want on the walkie-talkie is the guy who lives there. After all, his middle initial is "H."

That's my Theology of Purses 101. For the graduate course you'll have to make a trip to Canal Street for yourself.

This morning I got a call from a singer I've used on several of my jingles. She's struggling. She told me about this new show she wrote and produced.

"It's a strip show," she said, "But it's done in a burlesque style, so it's very classy, very sophisticated. We only go down to pasties." Okay.

Anyhow, she was looking for studio work, singing on jingles, whatever I might have for her. I told her that I'm doing very little on the commercial music scene these days, and more with writing books and speaking and stuff like that. She seemed surprised that I would walk away from a successful commercial music business, but was very interested in my new direction and asked about my book *Blue Collar God/White Collar God*. She was calling from the library and told me she would see if they had my book there.

"If they do, I'll check it out."

I wonder if this will be a story we hear more of later in the month. I guess my job isn't to finish all the stories, it's more important to start them.

After I hung up I was thinking about how my career has changed over the last few years and how that has happened. It might help you to understand this journal a little better if you knew the story behind this transition, so . . .

I did walk away from a twenty-year music career. And in some ways it wasn't easy. The money was a whole lot better than book royalties, at least at the rate that I'm currently generating book sales. Hanging out with creative types and amazing musicians—what's not to like about that? But there was that growing vacuum that I couldn't ignore.

I already told you about my "cow-pie epiphany" and how I looked back at all the commercials I had done. At how all my work so far had gone toward promoting things that could *improve* people's lives. Nothing, not one single thing I had ever promoted, had the power to *change* anyone.

That ended up being the pea under the mattress I could feel no matter how many layers were between it and me. It was growing, jabbing me in the ribs saying, "Don't let this comfortable music business lull you to sleep. There's something more you were created to do. Look for it."

Look for it? Where? I had no idea where to look. I was a music guy with a short attention span. Thirty-second songs were pushing it for me. I wasn't about to write a symphony.

But the next Christmas I got this idea to write an original carol, you know, four part harmony, lyrics that make you think about the real meaning of Christmas. So I did that. Then I printed it out on some cool, artsy paper and sent it out to several hundred people as part of our Christmas card. I sent it to clients, ad agency people, friends, family—everyone. In a sense, this was my "jingle for God," a subtle way of marketing the source of my joy.

And it scraped up some interesting responses. "Selling the Big Guy now, huh Esau?" "Cool Christmas jingle, man." And, "So that's what you think Christmas is about?"

It was fun, using my art to make people think about something a bit more significant than Handiwipes or the triple-stack pancake plate at Perkins. So I did it again the next year, and the next, and for six years straight.

On the seventh year, I pushed out the piano bench on December 15, because I'm nothing if not a good procrastinator. I sat there for a while, looking at the white and black keys. They looked back at me. Neither of us had anything meaningful to say to each other. But the whole time I was trying to conjure up an idea for a Christmas carol, I had a totally different idea running through my head. It wasn't a song, it was a story. I tried to push it away so I could write my carol, but it was persistent. Here's the idea that was running around in my head:

A guy wakes up on Christmas morning. He's disenchanted with his life. It's routine, dull, predictable — and what's more, Christmas has become that way too. The magic he used to feel in the season was gone. So he decides to do something a bit radical.

He takes a piece of cardboard and with a green magic marker he writes "Heaven," in big letters. He laces up his boots, throws on his coat, and heads out to the highway. He turns to face the oncoming traffic, holds up his sign, and sticks out his thumb and starts hitchhiking.

Before long he gets picked up by this guy in a rusted-out '88 Dodge Dakota dressed up, head to toe, like Santa Claus. He's just come from playing Santa at some party for fifty bucks. He doesn't look like a ticket to heaven, but our lead character hops in.

A few miles later they pull up to a stoplight and see another hitchhiker on the side of the road.

This guy is holding a sign almost identical to our protagonist—except his reads, "Earth." Santa says, "This I don't want to miss." He pulls to the side of the road, Mr. Heaven slides over, and Mr. Earth hops in.

So now we've got a guy trying to figure out how to get to heaven, sitting beside this Christ-figure who's "hitchhiking" to earth, and they're being chauffeured by Santa Claus who says, "I can't get you to heaven, but I can take you as far as the North Pole. Ho, ho, ho!"

Three crazies in the front seat of a pickup.

At this point I decided to get up from the piano and go write the story. There was no carol that year, but there was a quirky, sideways story about the search for meaning and the arrival of hope. That year the Christmas card included a story called The Hitchhiker.

Again, I got some interesting responses. "Nice Christmas, uh, story, man—hey, I thought you were a music guy." I did too, till now. Another person said, "Wow. That's a powerful picture of Christmas. If you believed that, that would pretty much change everything."

He used the "c" word. Change. Not improved or enhanced—changed.

I started writing more stories. I discovered that short stories were the literary equivalent of jingles. I felt like I already knew how to do it. And I uncovered a huge passion I had never noticed—I loved writing words. They felt so much like musical notes that I didn't even sense I was changing art forms.

And one other thing—this was fun. I was having a blast and had a growing sense of passion for what I was doing. Was I discovering a new direction for my life? Was this the "it" I was to look for? Was this what the pea under my mattress was trying to show me? I didn't know the answer, but I knew that something was right about all this. And it seemed logical to keep nosing down this path and see where it went.

Over the next couple of years I wrote about forty short stories. I wasn't exactly sure why I was doing it, I only knew that it felt right. Eventually that became the heart of my first book. Maybe this surprise journey began a long time ago.

I'm still nosing down this path.

But on to my day. Gotta keep writing, you know?

I needed to mow the lawn. Does it make sense to you that we fertilize our lawns, which makes them grow faster, which means we have to mow them more often? Some people love mowing the lawn. My dad, for example, is eighty-four, and he times himself when he mows to see how fast he can do it. That explains a lot about me; the muffler doesn't fall far from the chassis.

I've been looking forward to this day for a while. This afternoon my cousin and his wife from Cambodia are arriving at our house. They're going to spend several days with us while here in the US. They come back once every two years for a couple of months and we're lucky enough to get to hang out with them.

They run an orphanage, an AIDS hospice, a coffee shop/bakery, and a video production company over there. I'll tell you more about Tim and Dar tomorrow because we're going to be hosting a party for them at our house.

They called me from the edge of town just as I was hopping on my bike to do a quick ride, so I told them to meet me at the Caribou coffee shop in Wayzata. Tim and Dar are somewhere between coffee connoisseurs and coffee-holics. Maybe you have to be one to be the other, I'm not sure. Anyhow, we arrived about the same time and grabbed a table on the sidewalk. Mary and Lauren met us there a few minutes later and we had a fun reunion.

Tonight we had a party for our friends, Bob and Carin, who are moving to San Diego. The Steinies, who are also in our small group, hosted it. It will be sad to see them leave because it will leave a B & C-shaped hole in our group.

I love our group. I love the people in it. I wish you could meet them; they're an interesting bunch. And it's pretty odd how this group assembled in the first place.

A few years ago Mary and I would ride our bikes five miles early on Sunday mornings with these people over to Caribou. We'd sit for an hour and then ride home. Mary and I would then take quick showers and head to church. The other couples weren't really doing the church thing at the time.

One Sunday we asked, "Hey, why don't you guys come with us to church this morning?" They said, "Okay." They've been coming ever since. Once they started, there were lots of questions about God and religion and stuff, so we decided to extend our coffee experience to after-church as well. We reserved the back room of a coffee shop every Sunday, and once the service was over we'd go there and sit and talk about the questions that were raised during the service that morning.

It was really fun. That was three or four years ago, and we're still doing it. I'm telling you, this biking thing is a spiritual experience. At the very least, it leads there.

It's been an interesting day. From Purse Theology to strip shows to reminiscing about Christmas carols and Santa Claus to talk of Cambodia—it's all part of this "take a right at the next stairway and then left down the hall" adventure of life.

I'm sure glad I know the guy with the walkie-talkie.

DAY ELEVEN: DISPENSING HOPE

This was the day of the big party for Tim and Dar. I had sent out quite a few invitations. They were pretty blunt too. I told everyone that I was going to unashamedly ask them for money — unashamedly because I believe so strongly in what Tim and Dar are doing.

Mary and I went to Cambodia a couple of years ago to visit Tim and Dar and saw, firsthand, what they're doing over there. It was eye-opening.

We saw a hospital without doctors or nurses in what looked like a condemned, bombed-out, skeletal three-story building that opened into a "courtyard," which more accurately resembled a garbage dump, complete with rats who looked healthier than the people. The smell was as big a barrier to me as the sights. I've never smelled death so convincingly before. The rooms were filled; most of them with people dying of AIDS. Children, soon to be orphaned, were running along the corridors. We saw crying babies and a person trying to cook a malnourished fish over some coals in the hallway.

Tim and Dar picked up the children and talked to them, tickled them. They placed their hands on the foreheads of the dying and comforted them. I was nauseous. I'm not proud of that, but it's the truth. It was almost more than I could handle. Mary and I didn't say much, we mostly watched as Tim and Dar did their thing — offering comfort and love.

We left there and drove down one of the main roads of Phnom Penh. The road was lined with shanties made of wood, cardboard, and tin. It was around dusk. In front of these little shacks were little girls leaning against support posts trying to look brave. They were twelve or thirteen or fifteen years old. These were brothels, dozens of them. These little girls, children really, were preparing to "go to work." Their parents, trying to get enough money so they could keep the rest of the family alive with food, had sold many of them into prostitution. Most of these girls will have AIDS soon, and they'll pass it on.

I don't even want to write about this anymore. When you see it you just want to look away and go to your happy place. Unfortunately these people have no happy place. Many of them never have.

I guess that's why we're having this party tonight and unashamedly asking for money. We can't look away anymore.

Tim and I spent a good chunk of the day talking about the party and what we wanted to say and how. These Cambodian people lack hope. To them it's merely a word in the dictionary. Tim and Dar are trying to wrench the word from the dictionary and show them what it looks like in action. So tonight they're going to paint pictures of love and hope, to help the group see how they can offer these to the hopeless.

They'll paint a picture of the little huts they're building for people dying of AIDS to make their last days more comfortable. They'll describe how they talk of God's love and what it's like to tell these parents that when AIDS takes them, and it always does, their children will have a home at the orphanage and will be loved in the same way they have been loved.

Hope. Faith. Love.

This reminds me of a scene back in Soho, New York. We were walking down the street and saw a shop that looked abandoned. There was no signage on front, nothing to let you know what was inside. There were about forty female mannequins set back from the window aligned like soldiers marching in formation. I was curious, so I pushed on the door and it opened.

The place was huge, clean, gallery-like, and there was music coming from somewhere downstairs. Eerie music. Playing around, I told my daughters to go stand with the mannequins and pretend they were in the "supermodel military" and I would take their picture. That's about as far as we got because a security guard came over and yelled at me, threatening to take away my camera.

We walked down these huge stairs to what was evidently a retail area. There were large rooms with maybe three or four shirts or items of clothing in each. Either they were dangerously low on stock or they were taking minimalism to it's illogical extreme. I suspect it was the later.

We eventually found out it was a Prada store. Evidently this place is so beyond cool that you're supposed to instinctively know what it is. Putting signage on the front would be passé, so conventional. I guess they imagine their target customer to be the bourgeois vagrant who just wanders into spaces out of curiosity.

We saw a few shoppers. Nobody talked. I wonder if anyone bought. I never saw a register, a cashier, nothing like that. Maybe you're supposed to intuitively pay for merchandise.

The place gave me the creeps. There was a strange similarity here to Phnom Penh. Just like the twelve-year-old girls in front of the brothels, these women seemed to be void of expression. I saw no smiles, at least none that didn't look like lies. Blank eyes, heavy shoulders. The walls reeked of hopelessness. It was a bit hard to tell the mannequins from the "breathers." Had they threatened the employees with death if they showed any signs of life?

It scared me a little. Maybe our Americanized grasp on hope is more tenuous than we realize. Maybe we're vagrants, farther down the road toward lost than we know — nowhere is now closer than somewhere.

77

Maybe our affluence is anesthetizing us so we can't feel our lack of hope. We don't realize how close it is.

At least Cambodians have the excuse of a smorgasbord of obstacles to explain their hopelessness. Here in America we order it off the menu. We've created the dishes that serve it. We mix it with a lot of salsa so we can't taste it. What happens when we run out of salsa, when the anesthetic wears off? We'll be little girls with lost eyes leaning against support posts.

I don't like being such a "downer" in this. But it's just that the contrast is so stark between Cambodia and the US, between how Tim and Dar are spending their lives and how so many of us are frittering ours away. I know I'm generalizing here. I apologize to the scores of you who are selflessly investing your lives by loving people. But back to my generalization, somebody said that we Americans are on a "hedonistic treadmill." The concept of "more" is addictive, and we're full-fledged junkies. I hope we see that before we lose it — hope.

The party started at seven. I was a bit surprised at how many and who came. The first two to arrive were once-removed invitees — someone we had invited them. That's cool; we'll take anyone. We like those kind of surprises. Mary had put out a variety of drinks and appetizers and we all grazed for a while. Then, when the room was filled, we began.

As Tim and Dar were telling their story I looked around the room. These were good friends, people with good hearts, and most of them were wealthy. I will admit, I fantasized a bit about the potential of what could happen if we all came together and decided to do a good thing.

We saw a few short videos, heard a lot of stories, listened to a little history lesson of the Khmer people, and learned of a vision for the future. We let them all know how they could contribute. We had some dessert, some more talk, and then everyone went home. I have no idea how much money will be raised through this night. They are contributing directly so we are not in the loop, as it should be. I just hope it's significant for Tim and Dar and the Khmer people.

I rounded out the evening with the ultimate toe-stub of all time. This was a surprise I didn't see coming and would just as soon have never seen at all.

All of our guests had gone and Mary and I were talking with Tim and Dar in the kitchen. We had sequestered Bailey in Lauren's room for the evening, so now we set her free. She casually headed up the stairs to my studio where we had all met. None of us paid much attention to this till all of a sudden Dar screamed, "The desserts!" We had left all the desserts on the coffee table up there, and in .03 nanoseconds I pictured Bailey scavenging through it all, eating half and scattering the rest around the room like an explosion in Willy Wonka-ville. I took off sprinting through the family room and up the stairs, three at a time. As I got to the last three-stair leap, I turned, prematurely, to look around the corner to see how many desserts Bailey would have in her mouth. Big mistake! The last three-stair hurdle was only a 2 7/8-stair hurdle. I did a face-plant in the carpet, muffled a scream, rolled, grabbed the desserts, and hobbled back down the stairs. Did I mention that I was barefoot?

I set the desserts on the table and Tim, Dar, and Mary let out a collective gasp. I was bleeding like Old Faithful. Mary saw the blood and said, "You didn't get it on the carpet, did you?" This made Dar bust out laughing.

In Cambodia they must not worry about the carpet.

I was groaning like a wuss, wondering out loud if my toe was broken. The throbbing was keeping a good allegro tempo. After a minute or so we lifted the nail a bit to see what the skin looked like on the backside of the big toenail. A nice red shade of ugly.

Someone said, "Bailey, you're a bad dog." She cocked her head a bit as if to say, "Hey, that's transference baby. Don't blame me for Mr. Two

Left Feet's inability to navigate a set of stairs. I was just minding my own business, scrounging for a little sweetness."

I wasn't mad at Bailey. Not that I'm above that. She's collected my wrath for less direct involvement than this, but I think the pain drowned out my anger. It was holding my attention. There must be a threshold of pain that, when reached, supersedes and suppresses all other emotions and feelings. Evidently that threshold was reached.

The one question that did go through my head was, "Will I be able to bike?" Pathetic, isn't it?

So here I am, toe still throbbing (although it's now loping along at a comfy adagio), trying to wrap up my thoughts on the day. Frederick Buechner once said, "It's really very easy to be a writer—all you have to do is sit down at the typewriter and open a vein." I should be prolific tonight because I've got several started in my toe already.

All that downer talk from earlier, you would think I had popped a vein then. A lot of feelings have come out today. I think that's good, but at the same time, it can be rather draining. I think it was so much easier to write my first book—all I did was make up stories. I didn't have to dredge around in my own pool of feelings and lay it out there for everyone to see. This one is so much more personal, more blood and guts.

I'm enjoying it, I think, but I'm spilling more about who I am than feels comfortable. Maybe that's all part of the purpose here too, to walk where I'm uncomfortable.

Like down the hallway of that Cambodian hospital.

Sometimes the surprises are humbling, I think.

DAY TWELVE: THE WAH-WAH/FUZZ PEDAL

Tay had an early soccer practice today so I dropped her off at the field at eight. I ended up staying and talking with one of the dads, Dave, who also happened to be at our party last night. Dave's a good guy; George Clooney looks (so my daughters say) and a compassionate heart. He told me he was up most of the night, couldn't sleep. "I had wild dreams," he said. "Couldn't get the images of Cambodia and those children out of my head."

Dave was in no hurry. He had ideas on how to help. Sleepless nights are always good for idea generation. He listed things we could do, and offered suggestions on how to make these parties more engaging for people. I hope we can harness some of this enthusiasm and turn it into action.

Later, Mary and I took Tim and Dar to a place called World Market. They wanted to see what kinds of craft and art projects were being produced abroad and sold here. Dar is organizing groups of women to come up with salable items they can export to the US to help support villages and families.

While in the store I got a call from Robert, my French connection to cycling, who invited me out for a ride. I told him how I messed up my toe and wouldn't be riding for a while. Then Clint, the Lugermeister, called me. He's working on a cover design for the Surprise Me journal we're going to use at church. I talked to him about shooting a documentary of churches and other groups going through the Surprise Me experiment. That could be a pretty cool thing.

Which reminds me, Kurt—my friend who is the Mick Jagger of pastors—called and he wants to talk next week about his church, The Upper Room, doing the experiment. They are a church of about a thousand twenty-somethings. Lots of energy and passion. Hmm . . . sounds like a good group for a documentary.

Time for lunch at D'Amico with Tim and Dar. Tay and her buds showed up from cruising the lake. They looked like the cast of *The OC*. We've always called Brianna, our oldest daughter, the "bronze babe," but this week Taylor's the bronze one. Summer sun and boating have given her skin the color of the crust on butter-rubbed Tuscan bread.

Mary and Dar had some stuff to do, so Tim and I went cruising in my old Beemer convertible. We cranked up the oldies station, KOOL One-Oh-Eight. Blood, Sweat, and Tears came on with that seventies brass sound and David Clayton Thomas singing "You've Made Me So Very Happy." I took a few corners faster than I should. I wonder if anyone has ever done a study about music and driving? I swear I drive faster when the top is down and the music's up.

Then Tommy James and the Shondells started singing "Crystal Blue Persuasion." Tim began singing along. I joined in. There we were, two grown men singing oldies and car dancing—well, I'm not sure I'd call it dancing. If Tay had seen us she would have put herself up for adoption and told Tim he was no longer welcome in Minnesota.

This reminds me of a story—but then what doesn't? I was a senior in high school and it was time to place orders for our senior class rings. Remember those? Well, I wasn't really into rings; didn't need one, didn't want one. So I worked out a deal with my parents. I said, "I've been looking at this really cool wah-wah/fuzz pedal for my guitar. It costs less than a class ring. What do you say we settle on that and call it even?"

We did and I went in the basement, turned my amp up to eleven and wailed on "Crimson and Clover" by Tommy James and the Shondells.

Remember that song? It has a tremolo effect that sounds really cheesy now, but at the time it was too groovy for words. Way far out, man.

The next song on the radio was "Born to Be Wild" by Steppenwolf. Another one of my all time faves from high school. Another song that my wah-wah/fuzz pedal enabled me to emulate with more volume than accuracy.

In the seventies, distortion made prodigies of "no-talents" like me. Just the same, I was the biggest rock star in the basement of the house located at 502 9th Street, Mountain Lake, Minnesota, 56159. The walls loved me. They couldn't get enough.

The wah-wah/fuzz pedal changed my life. It gave me direction. I suddenly knew who I was. Okay, maybe I'm overstating things a bit, but it did reveal to me that creating sonic experiences was a way for me to get outside of my skin. It was self-expression that led to self-realization. I remember one day I went down into the basement to become "one with the pedal" only to find that my 9-volt battery had died. It was an identity crisis. I had to pawn an album to buy more juice for my foot-feed.

I wonder — what if my parents had never bought that wah-wah/fuzz pedal for me? Who would I have become? Where would I be today? Would I be a frustrated dentist trying to play melodies on the ivories of sedated patients? Would I be a Wall Street trader riffing on my exchanges like an operatic auctioneer? Was I one guitar-effects device away from grilling burgers at White Castle, sporting a T-shirt that says, "My other job is a Rock Star?"

The band America came on next with that meandering song "Horse with No Name." What does that mean? Nobody knows, including the guys who wrote it. Tim and I talked oldies and nostalgia. Remember In-A-Gadda-Da-Vida by Iron Butterfly? Seventeen minutes of vintage rock. I think I had every lick of that tune memorized.

All this reminiscing makes me think about turning points in my life that foreshadowed the "future of me." They weren't always the ones I suspected. They weren't always obvious. I never really thought buying the wah-wah/fuzz pedal was a defining moment for me, but maybe it was.

I wonder if I'll be collecting any defining moments during this Surprise Me month? I probably won't be able to answer that for a few years. It seems like time has to filter things before we know their significance, what really mattered.

Speaking of what matters, I need to confer importance onto this Spirit FM project right now and get this baby moving. I did. I spent three more hours on it while Tim parked himself on the hammock and played some Crosby, Stills, and Nash in his head. If I would have had my old trusty pedal, I think I would have done something "In A Gadda Da Vida-ish."

Mmmm. Kabobs, brushed with teriyaki sauce. Pedal or no pedal, my music making for the day was over.

Three hours of Spirit FM-ing was enough confer-ance of importance. Besides, Mary yelled up and said, "You better start the grill. The kabobs need to go on pretty soon."

Bri and Brian were coming over tonight. Mary's preparing a feast and we're eating out in the porch. We bought some super-sweet, sweet corn from this guy's vegetable cart on the corner. We're regulars of his. His name is Dennis, but we've taken to calling him Mr. Green Jeans. His corn is to die for. I'm not kidding. Mr. Green Jean's hybrid is one that makes God a little jealous. Mary lit a centerpiece filled with candles. She set a table that would have made the pre-prison, red jump-suited Martha green.

It was a perfect night. The sun filtered through the leaves, making the light dance across the table as the evening wandered on. Tim and Dar told stories. We all told stories. Then we did High/Low, where we go around in a circle and everyone tells their low point from the day, followed by a round where everyone tells their high point. Brian's high was from his morning reading of Oswald Chambers's devotional. It was about trust and God's timing. We all admit this can be a nebulous thing. Brian told about his struggles applying to law schools and the waiting and wondering that took place and how it stretched him and his trust threshold.

My high, as usual, was that very moment, sitting around the table together. Looking into the eyes of the people you love is about as good as it gets. Match that with teriyaki kabobs and good stories and you're looking at one happy puppy.

That was the day. My hair is still angled backward from flying in the convertible. That's one way you can tell if I've had a good day.

Oh, one more thing I wanted to tell you. Remember the guy I was talking about this morning, Dave, aka George Clooney, the one who couldn't sleep last night? Well, it's interesting how he came into my life.

I knew Dave casually, but one day he called me, out of the blue, and asked, "How did you get to where you are in your faith?"

A year earlier Dave had bought about a case and a half of my books and given them to friends for Christmas. A year later, he asked me this question. We talked for a while and then he said, "Well, the reason I bring this up is because I just decided to become a Christ-follower too." He told me how he had read my book last Christmas and knew there was something important in there so he gave it to his friends, but he never really took it for himself. Now he did.

He told me that he had made this decision about a month ago and hadn't really told anybody yet, but wanted to tell someone. I was so glad he did. It's exciting to see friends who have been on a spiritual quest for a long while put the pieces together and say, "Ah, I see. This is going to be so good!"

Friends. They enter our lives unannounced, and then they re-enter randomly. The way they trickle in and through our lives is so cool. They're like oldies songs. They keep showing up in our lives, and the longer it's been since we've heard their voice, the sweeter it sounds. The next thing you know you'll put the top down, start singing together, and drive a little too fast.

People are my favorite songs.

DAY THIRTEEN: CHANGE EVERYTHING

Today I've got to make music—lots of it. I wonder how God will surprise me on a day like this. I won't be around people very much. Mary's working all day, and I told Tim and Dar that I couldn't be their cruise director today. I can't even go top-down car dancing to oldies songs. Mostly, I'll be sitting in front of this computer and banging on a keyboard and guitar till the groove feels right or until my ears bleed—whichever comes first.

By the way, the toe hurts like a son of a gun today. There's no way I could wear shoes right now. Clown shoes, maybe. At least the rhythmic throbbing is gone. Now it's more like a drone—bagpipes of pain.

I spent a few hours working on a bluesy/retro/funk piece for the radio station, then took a break for lunch because I was all funked out. Sometimes food is the best transition from one musical style to another. I cruised over to Starbucks with Tim and Dar and we smoothied our way into a more jazzy state of mind.

We reminisced for a few minutes about our trip to Cambodia. I remember our daylong visit to the orphanage where we saw the first long-lasting smiles of our trip. These children seemed genuinely happy. They grabbed our hands and led us around, showing us their rooms, the gardens, the projects they were working on for school. They gave us a little show with singing and dancing.

As we were getting in the car to leave, one little girl, who had become Mary's shadow for the day, reached in through the open car window, gently touched Mary's arm, and very softly said, "I want you to be my mother."

How do you respond to that?

It was very quiet in the car for a while as we drove. I could see that Mary was feeling torn up over this. Who wouldn't be? Tim and Dar explained how they never adopt these children out to Americans, or to parents from any other country for that matter. They have a vision of rebuilding Cambodia from the ground up, and they think these children will be part of that vision. The orphans are learning about a loving God by spending time with loving people. They are being given that rarest of gifts in Cambodia — hope.

Tim and Dar dream of these children spreading love and being the seedlings of a new hope for this country. I know it seems unrealistic in many ways, an extreme long shot, but what are the options? It has to start somewhere. Wouldn't it be cool if a few generations from now a reborn Cambodia could trace some of its roots back to this little orphanage? Now that would be a cool surprise!

If you want to see a website packed with surprising love, check this out:

www.projectcambodia.com.

Back at my digital audio workstation, the music played on. Jazz with a melancholy leaning. I continued knocking out station IDs and themes.

Evening came, and Tim and Dar left to visit some friends. Mary was at work till nine, and Tay and Lauren, well, they have lives, social lives. I sat down to write a song for Taylor's sixteenth birthday.

This has become a tradition. I did this for our other two daughters when they turned 16, so Taylor had a pretty good idea that she was getting a tune. Actually I did it for Mary too, but it wasn't for her sixteenth. Let's just say it had a four and a zero in it, but that's all I'm telling you.

For Bri and Lauren I wrote songs from the perspective of me, Dad. It's nice, sentimental and all, but when you're sixteen and all of your friends are listening, I suppose it can be a little embarrassing. I thought maybe for Taylor I would just write a song as if it were a pop song about some girl named Taylor. You know, you turn on MTV and there's a music video about Tator Tot. So that's the direction I took.

I wrote a couple of verses and a chorus. Since we had just gotten back from New York and I had a lot of cool pictures of her walking down Fifth Avenue, I figured I'd make her a Big Apple girl. The video of Times Square at night will be cool with the music.

I made good progress on the music tonight. I edited a couple of cool orchestral samples and came up with the chord progression to drive the piece. So the outline for the song is all there. Maybe I can finish it tomorrow. I'll have to if I'm going to get a whole video edited together — by Monday.

I made a lot of music today. Days like this either make me miss my "old career" or they make me glad I'm out of it. Today was a little of both.

A few days ago I was writing about my transition from The Coast and the jingle biz to this new "writer of words" career. I never finished that story so here it is.

I told you about the six years of Christmas carols followed by the Hitchhiker Christmas story, then the forty short stories. I started finding increasing opportunities to tell my stories to people. Churches, retreats, colleges, high schools, book clubs — pretty much anyone who would listen. It was fun and very different than selling Prowl herbicide.

I was starting to find my feet in this new direction. I still wasn't making any money, but I had a creative outlet that fit who I was and the messages that I believed in — so, the money thing, I figured, would work itself out. Eventually.

Next step? Commit hari-kari on my advertising career. I'm not a good multitasker, never have been, so it's hard for me to have a divided focus. When I find a road that feels right, I like to barrel down it willy-nilly with abandon. I needed to get rid of my jingle-life, so I stopped selling myself to the advertising community. No marketing, no phone calls, no schmoozing, no nothing. My plan was to allow my music biz to atrophy over the course of several years and by the time it was on its last breaths, my new ventures would be sustaining us.

My theory seldom becomes my reality. I miscalculated a bit. Oh, my business atrophied all right, at about the pace I had anticipated; however, my new ventures, while growing, were not what I would call financially viable. I signed a publishing deal for my first book for what would be the financial equivalent of maybe doing a couple of jingles. The problem is, it's a whole lot harder and more time-consuming writing a book than a jingle. I don't think I can crank out fifty books this year. Nor would the forests of the earth want me to.

Finally, *Blue Collar God/White Collar God* arrived on the shelves. Leading up to that day, a lot of my friends asked me what I thought it would feel like to hold my book in my hand for the first time. I never gave it much thought till the day it arrived. I still remember every detail of it.

My publisher FedExed a copy to me as soon as the first run was completed. I remember getting that FedEx pack that day. I remember holding the package in my hand before opening it. I remember tearing the strip that opened the end of the package. I reached my hand into the box and paused. I took a breath — and pulled it out.

I looked at my book. I flipped it over and looked at the back. I fingered through the pages — and the weirdest thing happened.

I felt nothing. No excitement, no rush, no emotion — nothing. I actually got a little PO-ed with myself. "What is wrong with me?" I thought. "I should be excited about this. I should be jumping up and down. I should be dancing with this baby. I worked hard on this."

But still, nothing.

I didn't understand that day until several months later. I was sitting in my recording studio when Doug, my dentist, and the owner of a clinic down the street, walked through the front door. We don't really know each other very well, just the usual doctor/patient formalities. It's hard to have a long, meaningful discussion with your dentist — if you know what I mean. He was still wearing his scrubs and was very apologetic as he said, "I'm really sorry to barge in on you like this Terry, but have you got a few minutes to talk?" I said I did and he proceeded to tell me his story. Someone had given him a copy of my book for Christmas and he had set it on his nightstand by his bed. It sat there and collected dust for a month or so. One day he took it to Lifetime Fitness to read while he was working out. He finished it in a couple of days. Now, sitting across from me he said, "I just finished reading your book, and uh, I just wanted you to know that this is going to change everything." He paused. "I kind of grew up hearing about God and I suspected he was there, but he wasn't exactly part of my life. I didn't know that he wanted to know me — and wanted me to know him. What you're talking about in the book is personal, more like a relationship. I think this might change everything."

We talked some more. He told me he wanted to buy forty books and give them to his family and friends. Then he asked if I'd be willing to come talk to his employees. He was having a party for both of his offices, a post-Christmas party of sorts. He was renting out this bar and he wanted me to tell a story from the book and what it means to me. He wanted to give a book to everyone who worked for him.

We talked for a while, and then he left. I took a few deep breaths, my physical body searching for a way to process the emotions I was feeling. Then I got up and walked over to the fireplace in my office. I have this really cool, rustic, woodcut painting of Christ hanging above the hearth.

I stood in front of the painting, eyes watering, and I said, "The feeling that I didn't get when I saw my book for the first time—well I got that feeling now."

I wonder if God saved those feelings for this very moment?

The power of that moment with Doug is hard to describe. It was profound. It not only changed him, it changed me. In that moment I set the jingle business aside—for good. Not that there's anything wrong with being a jingle king. And I'm not saying that I'll never do more ad work, but my identity got a makeover that day. It was a turning point for me. I now saw myself as someone who wanted to spend the rest of my life involved in dispensing hope.

Like Tim and Dar.

The world is full of people like that little girl who asked Mary to be her mother. We all want someone to love us. We're all leaning in car windows looking to be adopted, accepted. And God is trolling neighborhoods looking for orphans. When he sees one, he throws his door open and says, "Hop in."

That's what I call a good surprise.

DAY FOURTEEN: SHOEBOB

Sunday mornings always seem more conducive to prayer than other days of the week. I know that's bogus and there's no evidence to support it, but still it seems true for me. Walking Bailey on Sunday mornings usually is a little less hurried so I get more face time with God. I tend to ramble on with him. But today, limiting myself to just those three words, "Surprise Me, God," seemed almost like I was getting cheated out of a deeply held liturgy.

I threw some other stuff out to God, out of habit. I hope that didn't taint the experiment. Rules — they're so stifling.

I put the coffee on for Tim and Dar before I left. The smell, I suspected, would pull their covers off and drag them into the kitchen.

As I was finishing my walk, I started thinking about a friend of mine, ShoeBob. He's a coffee-holic just like Tim and Dar. His real name is Bob, but we call him ShoeBob because he owns a shoe repair shop in Wayzata. According to him, he spends his days "saving soles." And he's good at it.

ShoeBob is a rather unassuming guy. No airs about him. No pompous persona. He's like Popeye, "I yam what I yam." And what he "yam" is a salt-of-the-earth guy who loves people and loves to make them laugh.

Eight years ago ShoeBob got an idea. He told everyone who walked into his shop that he was going to sleep outside in a tent, in December — in Minnesota, until he raised $7000 to help the homeless. People looked at him a little funny. "You're a shoe guy, Bob. What's with the tent and the concern for the homeless?" He raised over $10,000.

He did it again the next year, and the next. Last year ShoeBob slept outside till he raised over a million bucks! That's six zeros, baby. This year he's camping out for $1.25 million. And he'll get it. No doubt about it.

People believe in ShoeBob. He's a regular Joe who felt privileged and decided to do something for some other regular Joes who are less privileged. I think it's more about ShoeBob sometimes than it is about the homeless. People love ShoeBob and believe in his motives, so whatever he believes in, they believe in. Whatever he says is good, they assume is good. Who knew shoe repair guys wielded so much influence and power?

What would happen if some more visibly powerful CEO-type tried to pull this off? My guess is people would say, "I know ShoeBob, and you, sir, are no ShoeBob."

As Bailey and I rambled up the driveway, I thought, "Man, I wish I would have introduced Tim and Dar to this guy. They have such similar hearts. It would have been fun to hear their conversation."

As expected, they were sitting at the kitchen table worshiping a dark-roast bean when I arrived back from my walk. Tim and Dar were heading to Chicago in less than an hour, so they had already packed the car and were just waiting to say good-bye. I said, "I don't have to be in church for an hour; let's head over to Caribou for some real joe, and just hang out for a few more minutes."

As we were driving there I told them about ShoeBob and his story. I said, "next time you come, I want you to meet him."

We pulled up in front of Caribou and the first person to wave at me was ShoeBob. Surprise! We hopped out of the car and I introduced this "sole saver" who was showcasing his quirky, infectious grin. "Speak of the devil," I said, "ShoeBob in the flesh."

We got our bean and pulled up at a table outside with the Leather-man himself. A woman was sitting with him. Turns out she's the Twin

94

Cities chair for fundraising for some big Catholic relief organization. She's in charge of a $43 million dollar budget. S-s-s-surprise! She seemed very interested in what Tim and Dar were doing, and she and ShoeBob asked to be put on their e-mail list. I wonder if there will be an interesting end to this story?

After a few more minutes, Tim and Dar took off. I looked at ShoeBob and said, "Mary's working. Come sit with me at church so my daughter doesn't think I'm a pathetic loser." He humored me and came.

Paul, our preacher man, talked about being light. "Do you truly believe that you are the light of the world?" Matthew 5:14-16: "You are the light of the world . . . city on a hill . . . put your light on a stand . . . let your light shine before men so they may see your good works and glorify your father in heaven." I've been struggling a bit with this Surprise Me idea and it being "my" journal. I mean, who am I, anyhow. I'm just another guy. But, maybe this is just my way of letting my light shine. Maybe this is my stand that I'm putting my light on. That's all. Paul said, "Embrace your identity as light, then embrace your mission."

Maybe Surprise Me is my ShoeBob event, my mission. This is my version of sleeping out in a tent for a cause. It's possible. It's certainly a lot warmer.

Sometimes I wonder about the possibility of people misreading or misusing this experiment. Remember the Prayer of Jabez? A lot of people turned that into something it was never intended to be. God's not a maitre d' whose palm we can "grease" so we'll get the table by the window. Jabez became a genie-in-the-bottle approach for a lot of people. Not that it actually worked for them, but a lot of people turned that prayer into a mantra for health and wealth. "God, make my business flourish. Amen."

God wants to make "us" flourish. The business? Maybe — maybe not.

Surprise Me could have that same problem. And it probably will.

Some of us will only look for the sparkly toy surprises from the vending machine, the "good" surprises like the little gold rings and the rubber action figures. When a big dollop of "here's-what-I-see-in-you" comes rumbling down the chute, we'll go, "God, how come you're not answering my prayers? How come you're not sending any surprises my way?" All the while God is going, "Duh. I just sent a mirror down — did you look in it?"

So, that worries me a bit. Another thing that has me a bit concerned is that some of us will attribute everything that happens as an "act of God." You know what I'm talking about, right? Some of us will wake up in the morning and pray, "Surprise Me, God." And then we'll get a primo parking spot at the mall and the cell phone kiosk will have a special on the very camera phone we were thinking about buying and our son will hit a homer and win his Little League game and Ryan will get back together with Marissa on the OC and there will be *exactly* enough Bisquick left to make two pancakes and they'll be lowering the price of gas just as we're driving into the station and . . . And then we'll get together with some friends and in a religious voice that isn't our normal speaking voice we'll say, "Praise God — he is soooo good to me . . ." and we'll list the trivial train of "blessings." One of our friends who's trying to figure out this whole God/Jesus/faith thing will hear this litany of toy surprises and wonder why God just let her brother die of cancer. After all, she'd been praying for him as best she knew how for the past two years. Was God too busy helping someone get a good parking space? Is that how God works?

Surprise Me, the experiment, could do a lot of damage if we bastardize it; if we make it about us and what we want. God, I hope that doesn't happen.

You're probably thinking right now, "Okay, Esau, well then how are we supposed to know if anything that ever happens to us is actually from

God? What's from him and what isn't?"

You might not like this answer, but the truth is — I don't know. I'm not going to get into theology and stuff like that here. Dallas Willard or Ravi Zacharias or Greg Boyd can do that, but not me. I'm not that guy. I'm ShoeBob.

How could I know? How can we ever know, without a sliver of doubt, that whatever happened to us was a "God thing?" Unless he slaps a Post-it note on it that says, "This one's from me, you dimwit — I did it." But, the flip side to that is, just as we can't prove something is from God, we also can't prove that it isn't. We can't rule out his involvement.

So what do I say to the woman whose brother just died of cancer when she has been praying for him for two years? I don't know. I wish I could explain that, but I can't. That's a pretty awful surprise. Do I shoot out some clichéd line about how "all things work together for good?" Probably not. Do I put my arm around her and say "I'm really sorry about your brother — he was a good guy"? Yeah. That's a good start.

Other than that, I don't know.

This afternoon I went back to working on Taylor's song. It's actually going to be pretty cool. Hope that doesn't sound too arrogant; I'm just excited about how it's turning out.

I got a call from K J, a cycling buddy of mine who never works out and is still fast. I hate him for that. He told me he had talked to his neighbor who's also into cycling. K J was telling him about me, "there's this old guy I ride with," well, it turns out this guy's a musician I used to hire to play on commercials. He played with Prince for a few years. Killer keyboardist. K J said he's going to order my book. I'll have to connect with him and get him out riding.

Speaking of riding, I got out for my first one since the "toe incident." The toe wasn't happy, but after a couple of hours chasing Robert, my French-speaking Tour de France wannabe, I had pain everywhere so the toe was just another voice in the choir.

What a beautiful day.

Tay had a truckload of friends hanging at our house, but I kicked 'em out so I could work on her song some more. At eight Mary got off work and called me. We met at D'Amico for dinner and some face time.

My wife, by the way, has a great face. I wish I could see more of it. It recovers so well from the swings of life — between the good stuff and the hard stuff. It's seen great joy and great pain, but it always bounces back. It's still one of the freshest faces I know and the one I never get tired of.

Speaking of tired, I am. I'm hauling this face to bed.

DAY FIFTEEN: TAYLOR'S SONG

Monday, Monday . . . I'm on my way to a recording studio to cut the vocals and mix the song for Tay's music video.

First surprise? I got lost on the way there. Once I found the address of the studio, I rang the bell out front and no one answered. I walked around to the back door and pounded. No answer. Finally I just walked in and went down into the basement. There they were, waiting for me to arrive. Soundproofing has its downside.

It was a cool little basement studio. We got right to work and knocked it out in a few hours. By the way, here's how the lyric ended up. Remember, the idea was to write a song you might hear on the radio — not a "Daddy-loves-his-baby-girl" kind of song.

Every Time (Taylor's Song)

Written by Terry Esau ©2004

Every time I turn around
I see her on 5th Avenue
She's the girl that turns my head
And makes me wonder why

Every time I see her smile
I can't remember what to say
I look into the ocean of her eyes
And drift away

Chorus

My Taylor's made for sunshine
She's always dancing in the rain
My Taylor's made for laughter
And she's the girl that knows my name

Every time she falls asleep
A million stars just wait for her
And when she opens up her eyes
The sun comes out to play

Every time she makes me mad
She melts me with that funny grin
And when I hold her in my arms
I know the world's okay

Bridge

Every time I turn around (4xs)

Every time I touch her heart
She knows just what I'm going through
Angels aren't supposed to cry
But sometimes they still do

Chorus

Every time I turn around
I see her on 5th Avenue
She's the girl that turns my head
And makes me wonder why

As we were cutting the vocals, we had some minor problems with pitch. Mark, who was singing the song, was not used to singing at nine-stinking-a.m. on a Monday morning, and why would he be? Nobody does vocal sessions at that time — nobody in his right mind, that is. So, we'd get a line that felt right, but had some pitch issues. Then we'd get one where the pitch was cool, but the feel wasn't quite happening. Finally the engineer said, "Let's throw some Auto-Tune at it."

Auto-Tune is a program that takes a track and rounds errant pitches up or down to the nearest true pitch. In other words, it makes it sound like you sang in tune even if you didn't. I've never been a big fan of this technology. Early versions of this program were a bit uneven. Also, engineers with bad ears would overuse the program and make tracks sound artificial and mechanical.

This, however, was a newer version of the program, and the engineer knew how to use it in a subtle way that sounded natural and real. I had been a little too eager to toss out the less-than-perfect tracks and just keep trying to get it right. The engineer finally convinced me that we had what we needed, it just needed the loving, tender touch of Auto-Tune to make it beautiful.

And he was right. When used properly, he was able to forgive errant pitches while leaving the personality of the track unaffected.

As I was driving home, I was thinking about my life — the "Monday-morning-off-key-vocal-track" that is me, my voice, my life. If God wasn't such a loving music producer, he would have tossed out my tracks with a "This guy just can't sing in tune" dismissal. But he values the "personality" of my voice, so he runs me through Auto-Tune, through Auto-Forgive. Instantly the track of my life is in tune. My song is worth listening to again.

If he was a producer like me, he'd probably just keep hitting the red button, saying, "Is it too much to ask you to sing one flippin' line in tune?

Gosh!" And I'd probably keep trying and keep failing. Pretty soon I'd get frustrated with my inability to sing in tune and say, "Forget this. I can't sing in tune. Why try. I'm evidently not a singer. I'm done trying. I'm done singing." And I'd walk out of the studio and never come back.

God doesn't want that. He made us all to be singers. He made us all with very cool voices. We just have pitch problems, that's all. We need a touch of his Auto-Tune.

Here's the cool surprise in this—God keeps showing me illustrations of his grace and forgiveness. I keep finding images of redemption in the strangest places—even in signal-processing programs for recording studios. God is pretty creative at delivering messages to us that are personalized, in ways that make sense to us. Think about it, I've spent my whole career working with singers to get the "perfect take." Who better, and how better to teach me about my inability to achieve perfection and my need for grace? It's a tailor-made lesson just for me—no pun intended.

Back home, I sequestered myself in my studio with iMovie. iMovie is a Mac program for editing video clips and photos together with music to make, in this case, a music video for my Tator Tot. I had never touched this program before but jumped right in and started editing as if I knew what I was doing. It probably would have been wise to read the manual first, but nah—winging it is more fun.

By mid-afternoon I was thirty seconds into the edit—pretty good progress for a neophyte.

My editing was interrupted by screaming downstairs. I ran out of my studio and found Taylor and Chelsea covered, like ballpark hot dogs, in catsup and mustard—gasping for breath. The only thing missing was some good sauerkraut and relish. The girl's soccer team had evidently gone to Costco and bought the industrial-sized bottles of catsup and mustard and planned a sneak-attack on the boy's soccer team.

This was a flawed plan from the get-go. Girls need to understand that boys are genetically more skilled at war games. And there's nothing they love more than a playful war with the opposite sex, especially one that involves squirt bottles and condiments. What's more, boys don't really mind being "nicked" with the Heinz sauce, as long as they know the girls will be doused in it.

And they were. Evidently it was only a matter of seconds before they stripped the girls of their weapons and gave the weaker soccer-ettes mustard shampoos. Besides that, the boys had been planning their own secret attack. They had gone in search of some nice, ripe roadkill, as in dead, rotting raccoons and crows. They sent some guys to deliver the carcasses to the interiors of the girls' cars while the fracas was going on.

They also found a dead carp. It turns out that you can wield a carp like a whip and flog girls with it. How fun is that? They carp-whipped and condiment-hosed the girls back to their roadkill-filled cars and sent them whimpering home to their dads in their stink-mobiles. Sometimes I really miss being a teenage guy; they get all the fun.

Tay and Chelsea squish-squashed their way up to the shower and lathered away the c & m. (For days, every time they passed me I got the strangest craving for an Oscar Meyer hot dog.)

Maybe it was all the smells that motivated our mutt to want to get into the act, but Bailey, our girl-dog that sometimes acts like a soccer boy, snuck out of the house and found some road kill of her own and proceeded to roll around in it. She came back smelling worse than the entire girls soccer team. I wish I could Auto-Tune that mutt! This whole day seems to be about the smell of death slathered in catsup and mustard. Mary graciously hauled Bailey to Petco and handed the furry stink bomb off to them to clean. I hope she tipped them well.

Tonight I climbed back up to my studio and worked on the music video edit till 1:30 a.m. I only got a little over a minute into the song before the drowsiness started taking a toll on my thinking. I was starting to thurn tings around so I decided to quall it cits and bo to ged. (Sleep deprivation dyslexia.)

Even though I was in dreamland, the soccer war had not been put to rest. The whole girls team was doing a sleepover at the Meyer's house and had made plans for late-night revenge — of the TP variety.

At 2:30 a.m. they snuck through the woods, cases of toilet paper in hand, up to the Nydan house. This is a family with five boys, two of whom were on the boy's soccer team. These two were possibly the most deserving of revenge since they had been on the front lines with coons, crows, and carp.

The girls were about to fire the RPCs — rocket-propelled Charmin — when the lights in the garage came on, blinding them. All they could see was the silhouetted profiles of the Nydan brothers, standing in the garage in full combat regalia, walking casually toward them, Freddy Kreuger style, paintball rifles in hand. You guessed it. It was a colorful night under the moonlight. Nobody got TP-ed, but some behinds got a fresh paint job.

The brothers managed to kidnap one of the girls, Colleen, and brought her into the garage and Saran-Wrapped her till she couldn't move. They put her under the light so the girls, who had fled to the cover of their cars, could see this poor thing that was now a POW in the Nydan camp. They called my daughter's cell phone (makes me proud to know that she played such a key role in the negotiation process) and convinced the girls to drive up the driveway to work out a deal. With doors locked and windows barely cracked, the Camp Nydan talks were initiated.

Somewhere in the middle of this international diplomacy, the boys slid a car jack under the rear end of the car and in seconds jacked it up so the wheels were no longer touching the ground. Who were these guys, backup pit crew for Jeff Gordon? Now the negotiating had definitely swung in favor of the Axis of Evil.

The girls decided to pull out the big guns. They batted their eyes at the boys and threatened to cry. Well, that's like Kryptonite to the male species. It's cheating. We're helpless. After a few minutes the boys set them all free. After all, it had been a good day for their platoon. The girls had been decorated in paint, coons, crows, and carp — a nice collection of crap. Score: Nydans-4, Girls-Nil. The boys decided to call it a night.

Well, not just yet. After the girls went back to the Meyers to sleep it off, the boys picked up the Charmin that had been discarded in the rapid escape and did a little tree trimming at the Meyer's house. TP-ed to high heaven.

I'm kind of glad I didn't know all this was going on, and yet, I'm kind of jealous. Why don't adults TP the houses of friends? Why don't we kidnap each other anymore? We get so serious and so responsible. Practicality and logic — boring! We should get at least one day a month where we get a pass to act like juvenile delinquents. Well juveniles, at least.

I remember Mary telling me once that she wished our house would get TP-ed. When I asked her why, she said because that would send a message to our daughters that somebody was thinking about them. You don't TP someone who's not on your radar screen. In a strange sort of way it's a twisted compliment. It's a variation of flirting. It's affection that requires cleanup.

She's right. Our maples and oaks have been trimmed several times over the years, and on none of those occasions did our girls cry or complain. A smile crept across their faces, even though they knew they'd have to spend hours pulling the Charmin from branches.

Maybe this Surprise Me thing is God's way of TP-ing my life. I secretly want my world to be hit with his streamers. It lets me know that

I'm on his radar screen. He's flirting with me, showing affection. Is it always beautiful? Not really. But that depends a bit on how I look at it. There's nothing particularly attractive about toilet paper hanging from trees, but if you squint and take a panoramic view, there is a certain charm to the Charmin look. All the surprises coming into my life this month aren't necessarily beautiful, but I can probably find beauty in them if I squint and step back to see the big picture.

It's clear that Taylor had more of a Surprise Me day today than I did. She got the works. I wonder if she prayed the prayer this morning? I think we learned some things today . . . .

1. Boys are better at war games . . .
2. Payback is always more severe . . . .
3. Boys and girls love this dance they do . . .
4. I'm a little jealous of the dance.

I think I'm going to do more dancing with the people in my life. My wife, my girls, my friends, my God. I want to TP their lives and let them know that they are on my radar screen. I want to sneak up and randomly drape their trees with affection.

Also I'm going to wake up every morning and walk to the window to check the trees of *my* life. I'm going to look for traces of Charmin in my days. I'm going to step back and enjoy it, whether it's pretty or not.

DAY SIXTEEN: THE PARTY

Today is Taylor's sixteenth birthday. Surprise! How in tarnation has my baby girl arrived at sixteen years old? Somebody's been messing with time, and if I get my hands on 'im, ooh baby . . .

We, Mary and I, have been planning a huge surprise party for Tay tonight. Her friends have been clandestinely spreading the word about the party, and so far I don't think she's got a clue. Of course we're always the last to know anything. Her friends told us to expect seventy to eighty kids. Hello! Well, here's how the day looked leading up to the party.

We called Tay on her cell phone at 7:30 in the morning to sing and wish her happy birthday. She had slept over at a friend's house and was now on her way to soccer practice. She was groggy, with a capital "GROG." The birthday hadn't sunk in yet — consciousness was barely afloat.

I took the stairs to my studio — three at a time — including the last three. I was one minute into editing her three-minute music video. Lots of pictures left to download and arrange just so. This editing thing is time-consuming, but fun. I get to relive some of the fondest moments of her life, and mine, as I look over the photos. It's a breakneck-pace race down memory lane.

Tay came home after soccer and slept for a while between her two practices. I edited some more, with the volume on low. Then she had her second practice from noon to 1 p.m. I picked her up after that and we met the fam at D'Amico's for lunch. Mary, my girls, and me — chowing Italian food in the sunshine on our baby's sixteenth birthday. I felt like

I'd died and gone to Italy . . . er, heaven.

Came home and . . . edited some more. I finished the last frame at 4:30 on the nose. I asked the computer to render the video and it looked at me like, "Hey bub, haven't I done enough work for you in the last twenty-four hours?" It was going slow. I mean really stinking slow. My iMac finally finished "thinking" about 5:20. We were all heading for dinner at Benihana at 5:40. I was concerned, "What if something went wrong on the DVD burn and we get back here with seventy kids and I pop the video in and . . . nothing. That would be a bummer."

The burn happened pretty fast. At 5:36 it finished and I popped it in the DVD player and, voila, it worked. Whew!

Went to Beni's and had a blast. This is one of those places where we all sit around this big flat grill and the samurai-ginsu dude does a choreographed dance with knives and shrimp and chicken and rice and veggies that he slices and dices mid-air. Lots of aerobatics. I swear I don't know how the food gets cooked because it spends more time in the air than on the grill.

But we don't question his culinary wisdom, his techniques, or even his taste in seasoning. You just don't criticize a chef who could trim your eyelashes mid-blink.

Senshu, our performance-art chef, bowed to us, then left us to our gift-opening.

Tay got some great gifts from us, if I don't mind saying so, and some cool stuff from her buddies Alex, Bryn, and Courtney. I snapped the camera multiple times so we can relive this slash 'n sear birthday bash for many years to come.

We drove back home to a house that, by now, should be packed to the gills with schools of Taylor's buds. As we came around the block, there were cars everywhere. I casually said, "Hmmm, the Pettis's must be having a party." I tried to be cool about it, but I could see that Tay was recognizing a few cars. They weren't big SUVs or four-door-grown-up-looking-cars — they were old rusted-out Honda Civics, the kind parents buy for newbie drivers.

We pulled into the driveway. The house appeared to be swaying a bit. Maybe it was my imagination. As we got out of the car, I didn't say much. It was a little late now to feign innocence or to try to pretend there wasn't a dragon under the blanket when you could see the whole tail sticking out. As Tay reached for the doorknob, she looked back at me with a look that said, "Soooo Daddio, you been up to something?"

The door opened, the "Surprise!" rang out, Taylor blushed, and the party was on. There were lots of hugs and kisses. I made a mental note of all the boys that engaged in that friendliest sort of greeting. The music pumped, laughter echoed, and I believe I saw the twins, Peace and Quiet, slip out the back door while the Nydan brothers swaggered in the front. Yesterday they were "carp-whipping" my baby — today they came bearing presents. Evidently there's a mandatory truce in soccer wars to make way for surprise parties. Mary got the food going and I became a courier of bottled water and various sodas.

Have you ever noticed how when it's really, really loud someplace, you can get lost in the sound? It's like after a while the noise becomes silence and you can almost hear yourself think. All the laughing and talking and music and stuff cancel each other out till there's nothing. I was walking around delivering drinks and food in a vacuum — a slow motion, silent vacuum.

It was an out-of-party experience. You've heard about those, right? I'm floating above the crowd, observing, enjoying the whole scene. I saw Taylor's friends laughing and honoring her with their words and presents. I saw Mary serving everyone, trying to make them comfortable and happy — and I knew she was doing all that because of her love for Taylor. I saw the joy and life in the room and it made me feel really good. It was like I was seeing all this and going, "Yeah, this is what I had envisioned. This is what I wanted. I love Taylor and she is the object, the focal point of that love right now." My out-of-body face smiled.

Okay, so here's my Surprise Me revelation du jour. You knew it was coming, didn't you?

I wonder if this whole Surprise Me experiment is like God throwing us a surprise party? Here's how it looks to me.

He's looking down from his "out-of-body" perch, and he sees me and says, "You know, I love that Terry dude. I'd like to throw him a party to show him how much I love him. I'll call him and sing to him how much I love him. Yeah, and maybe I'll write a song for him and do a music video. Some presents, that would be good. Oh, and I'll get some munchies and drinks and we'll all hang out together and laugh and tell stories and tell him how much he means to us. Yeah, that'll be fun. I'm gonna do it."

So he does. He plans and prepares and creates and orchestrates a great party for me—a party called Today. And I wake up on the day of this party. My eyes crack open. Light streams in. I yawn. I look over at Mary as the sun peaks through the window and sparkles and dances on her hair. The birds outside our window sing—and I wonder if that's God's voice singing along with them.

I sit down at the computer and write some words that feel melodic and true, words that come from my heart, or someplace even deeper—and I feel like he has written a song for me, through me, with me.

At lunch I order a muffeletta and a rhubarb crustata for dessert. The first bite of each is heavenly. And I hear the chef in the kitchen saying, "Is Terry enjoying the rhubarb? You know, he's one of the reasons I created rhubarb in the first place—I knew he'd be crazy about it." And the God of taste buds smiles as he watches me savoring his rhubarb through the crack in the door.

I meet with friends, they call me on my phone, they yell to me from across the street when they see me passing. "Hey Terry. See you at the soccer game tonight. Save me a place, will ya?" And the God of friends says, "I've given you some really good ones."

I hop on my bike and cruise some winding, tree-covered roads that snake around lake Minnetonka. I love wraparound sight, peripheral vision when I'm riding. It feels like I'm inside the acetate reel at an omnimax theater. I finish the ride as I fly up our driveway under a canopy of tree branches — oaks, maples, ironwood, ash, balsam — and I feel like I've just traveled within a virtual reality video by God, with God, from God.

We go out for ice cream after the game, just me and my girls, my family. We sit around a table and process the game, process life, and process love. We smile and hug and laugh. And as I look in the eyes of my wife and my girls, the God of bow-wrapped presents says, "Wow, I've given you some really great gifts, if I don't mind saying so myself."

As my surprise party comes to an end, I walk Bailey out into the silence and look up at the remnants of the day's party, the twinkling starry decorations scattered across the sky. I hadn't seen them earlier because the video was showing and the music was playing and my friends were my focus. But now, under the Milky Way, I see them and hear him say, "You are loved. Even when you don't feel it or believe it, you are loved. I put this party together for you today because you are just that important to me. Surprise!"

And guess what? Tomorrow when I wake up, he does it all over again. Another surprise party, for me. He sings to me again. He gives me more presents. He tells me he loves me.

The noise of Taylor's party comes cymbal-ically crashing back into my consciousness and I somewhat reluctantly rejoin my body.

Oh, I haven't told you how Taylor's surprise party ended. The music video. I was a little nervous for this because I had worked so hard on it and I really wanted her to love it. I guess if I even looked deeper than that, I wanted her to understand how much I loved her. We managed to get all seventy or eighty kids to quiet down, and I hit the play button. All eyes were on the TV monitor for three-plus minutes. Many of them saw pictures of themselves in the video. There was some laughing, some pointing, "That's me, that's me!" And then it ended. It was eerily quiet. Nobody said anything. Then Tay got up, very deliberately, stepped over the people on the floor, and walked up to me and gave me a big hug. I melted. I felt like I had just won an Oscar. I know she was thanking me for the present of the music video, but what I felt was more than just that. I knew I was being hugged by one of God's greatest presents to me. A present he gave Mary and me — a present we unwrapped at a surprise party he threw for us exactly sixteen years earlier.

It's funny, isn't it, how making our kids happy, makes us happy? I suppose God must feel that way too. Well, tonight we had a whole chain reaction of happiness going on. Taylor ripped open the obvious presents, but there were presents everywhere. They *are* everywhere. And tomorrow morning I get to wake up, I hope, to another surprise party that my father has planned for me. I'm going to keep my eyes open; maybe I'll see familiar cars parked around our block, or the walls of our house swaying, or . . .

DAY SEVENTEEN: MIDNIGHT BLUE

Two slices of thick-cut English-muffin bread, some black cherry jam, a Sunkist orange, and a glass of grape/apple juice. Iams vitamin-enriched dog food. My breakfast. Bailey's breakfast. Glad I'm not a dog. Still, she molarizes those dry smelly chunks like they're 'Toblerone nuggets. Cuisine contentment — she's got it, I don't want it.

"Surprise Me, God."

It's the morning after the night of the big surprise party for Taylor. Just thinking about it makes me smile. As I was eating, I spread out all of Tay's birthday cards in front of me on the kitchen table. I read a card, took a bite, read a card, took a bite — responsive eating. One theme kept popping up in her cards, "Tay, you're such a great friend to me. You're kind and caring. I always know I can trust you. You treat me good."

I love that. She's become a well-oiled relational machine. Life is like black cherry jam once you've figured that out.

Is it common that the day after a "big deal day" is not much of a day at all? That's how it feels so far today. It's almost noon and it doesn't seem like God's in the mood for a surprise party. I know I shouldn't be relying on feelings, but just the same, he doesn't feel very present. Maybe I shouldn't be questioning his presence . . . or his presents, for that matter. Still, he feels silent. The world feels silent. My friends are silent. My family is silent.

I wish my mind was silent. Instead it's yakking at me, almost accusing me, questioning the value of "my little game." "Where's your surprise party now, chump?", Come on, God, do your thing. Pick me up, cheer me up, make me happy . . . surprise me.

Silence.

What's that all about? Sometimes it feels like God loses his voice. He becomes a mime—on radio. I suppose it's possible that his voice is fine and I've just lost my hearing.

Or, what about this idea—when we're a little down, things aren't going our way, and life is hard, we *think* that God is silent. What if that is the very time when he is yelling his lungs out?

We know that we learn more, grow more, and mature more through the tough times in life, yet we assume that those are the times when God is silent. Kind of counterintuitive, don't you think? If he's so silent, how is it that this is the time when we learn the most, grow the most? Why do we value those times so much—after they're over and done? Why do we instinctively know that it was a good thing for us to go through that dark silence?

I think God is a painter, and midnight blue is his favorite color. He loves spending a good chunk of his paint budget on those moody, dusky, dark shades. Then, all of a sudden, like a crazy man, he splashes some bright reds and yellows in just the right places, and suddenly, we understand. If he had started with the reds and yellows, would we have understood? The night explains the day. The bleak interprets the bright. The dark illumines the light.

Life is spectral, a physical, mental, emotional, and spiritual spectrum. A colorfest. If life were all red—only red, then red would be the new black. But red would get old, dull, and gray. Then when black finally came along again, we'd go, "Where have you been all my life, blackie? You make red look so, so, yesterday." And black would be the new red.

Here's the point, I think—God has a big palette. He has lots of colors, and he knows how to use 'em. We need to trust the Painter with his colors.

He'll make something of our canvas. He always has, always does. Listen during the silence—*especially* during the silence. He's probably yelling.

He still seems silent today, and I still don't like it. Maybe I'm a color-blind, artistic ignoramus. Gimme some red and I'm happy.

I got a last-minute call for a lunch meeting with Dave, an old friend.

I guess God got tired of midnight blue for a second. Good.

Dave was surprised when he got a two-hour lunch break, unexpectedly. He's a surgeon and this never happens. We had a great conversation. We talked about letting go of our kids and the concept of "premature rescue"—you know, saving our kids before they have a chance to save themselves. He told me how his wife sometimes does this with school projects. The kids "remember" on Sunday night about a project due the next morning so she saves them by running to Target, getting some poster board, and sitting around the table till late working on it, all the while lecturing their child on promptness and responsibility. Instead, should we let them fail, get a bad grade, with the hope they will learn a more valuable lesson of life?

I just got back from lunch and my mind flipped back to the color thing, and God's apparent silence. What do you think of this: Maybe if he was too quick with the reds, he would be prematurely rescuing us. You know, stunting our growth by being an over-eager parent. God is saying, "You know, I could run to Target for you tonight, get some poster board and swish some red paint on it for you, but that wouldn't really help you in the long run. No, I think I'll just let you fail. I know, it's not fun, but I think it will protect you from a bigger failure down the road. Trust me, midnight blue is what your canvas needs right now."

So, that might feel like silence to us, but I don't think it's an absence of involvement. When we as parents don't rescue our kids, it's not because we don't hear or care. It's almost the opposite. And it is for him too. He's looking at the big picture. We're thinking micro, he's thinking mural.

Another thing. If you're a parent, you know how hard it is to let your child fail. It's unbelievably painful. That's probably why we step in so often, prematurely. We can't handle the pain. This is where God is a better parent than we are. I suspect he feels that same pain at watching us fail, watching us fall, but he sees down the road and opts for the course that leads to our greater good. I wonder if he sometimes cringes when he dips his brush in the midnight blue?

God trusts us to learn and grow with minimal coercion. He has an economy to his brush strokes. He doesn't slap us with colors we don't need. You've seen those "starving artist" paintings? Sometimes it looks like they're painting in all capital letters. Overblown. Overkill. Over-oiled.

God, the Picasso of humanity, makes no such mistake. Every stroke is precise, critical, perfect.

Thankfully, for me and you, a phone call interrupted my paint-by-number theology. It was Dutch, one of my roommates from college who lives in Atlanta. He told me that he had gotten a call from his pastor. His pastor told him the painful story of just finding out that his high school-age daughter was pregnant. They were distraught. Their pastor wanted to be very upfront about the situation with the church, so he is going to make it public on Sunday. He asked Dutch to give a response from the elder board. (Are you thinking what I'm thinking? It seems the only "response" necessary would be a tidal wave of love and support.) Dutch called to get my thoughts on how he might handle the situation.

Dutch is one of the most humble and least self-righteous people I know, so he's perfect for the job. I told him not to play to the guilt-giving minority, but to assume that the church will be givers of grace.

I half-joked and said he should get up and confess that he gossiped or something like that in the past week and ask the church to forgive him. Then, at the end, casually, as if an afterthought, throw in the other story as if it's a side-item and suggest the church be equally forgiving in that situation. Whatever Dutch does, I'm sure it will be real, authentic, and saturated in grace.

So then, D K stopped by, my Polish homie. This was a bona fide surprise. I haven't seen him in ages. D K designed and built my last recording studio. Remember, The Coast, I think I told you about it earlier. He's this guru carpenter/musician/creative crazy man—my kind of guy. He moved to Florida a few years back and we've pretty much lost touch. He told me he had read my book and then gave it to a friend. He told me he still doesn't necessarily believe in God but he enjoyed the book. Said he could see me as he read it, it sounded like I was sitting there talking to him. He's still struggling with depression, but now that he understands it better, he's more equipped to pull himself through it. There's that midnight blue again. God is trusting D K to learn from it, and I believe he will and is. I suspect the brush is poised and about to be dipped into the red.

The day is winding down. Sometimes that's a good thing. One more event. Deep breath.

It's the soccer end-of-season pool party at Pat and Julie's house. My friend Keith, dad of one of the girls on the team and a guy that I coached the girls with for many years, gave all of the girls a T-shirt that said, "Hooah!" It's a cheer taken from the military that signifies approval, encouragement. We do it all the time during practices to encourage the girls when they do something out of the ordinary or give an exceptional effort. Sally will do one of her textbook sliding tackles and we'll yell, "Everybody, let's give a Hooah to Sally—one, two, three—Hooah!" They yell it, they love it.

Do you suppose God goes Hooah for us? Is he cheering for us when we do well or just give an exceptional effort? I hope so. He says he's our father, and he wants to coach us, so in a way he's a "dad-coach" just like Keith and I are. We always looked for excuses to Hooah the girls. It's fun to see the proud grins on their faces when we all cheer for them. My guess is that God is at least as generous with his Hooahs as Keith and I are.

Sometimes the girls on the team would beat us to the cheer. They'd see one of their teammates make a great play and one of them would just yell out, "One, two, three . . ." and a thunderous Hooah would echo off the back wall of the school. As coaches, we especially loved it when they did that. It created great team spirit. You know, I bet God is like that too. Even though he loves cheering for us, he loves it even more when he sees us learning the principle and we start Hooahing each other, randomly, raucously.

God knows the world could use a little more Hooahing.

So, go Hooah somebody who's having a ho-hum day. Make the neighborhoods echo, people. It's good for team spirit.

Considering that the day started with me feeling that God had laryngitis — you know, the cat had his tongue, well he's turned out to be pretty chatty after all. My ears are ringing.

I think I'll find the pillow and watch the midnight blue fade to black.

DAY EIGHTEEN:
KITCHEN CONVERSATION

Surprise Me, God."

I'm meeting Riggins for the last time today. He leaves for UCLA tomorrow. He just finished reading *Blue Like Jazz* and told me he bought another book, *Jesus Among Other Gods*, by Ravi Zacharias, and he wants us to read it together and discuss it while he's at college. Great idea. I'd bet God helped him find that book. I hope. We discussed parents, expectations, life, etc. again. Hugged.

Lanie, a singer/songwriter friend of mine, called and asked if she could bring her niece over. She's visiting from Nevada and saw *Blue Collar God/White Collar God*, in Lanie's son's room and started reading it and asked where she could get her own copy. Lanie said, "I know exactly where we can get it." So they came over and we talked for a while. She also told me that her son was reconnecting with God — he's much more interested again. There's another guy I want to connect with in the next few weeks.

I finished doing the Spirit FM edits and mixes. Tomorrow I do all the vocals and final mixes and mastering. There's roughly a 100 percent chance that I'm being optimistic about how much I'll get done. Either way it will be a looong day. Wish I could watch the opening ceremony of the Olympics.

Had lunch with Taylor today, and I told her that I had read all of her cards and was impressed by how many of her friends trusted her and respected her. She didn't say too much, but I think she appreciated being affirmed. That was sort of a subtle Hooah.

Her music video is turning out to be quite the hit. Last night at the soccer party they showed it about eight times. Not sure if Tay is embarrassed or proud—maybe both.

On my ride today I came up to a thirty-ish woman who was slogging along against a pretty good headwind. I slowed and talked to her for a while—thought I should open the surprise portal and see if anything lumbered through. Nothing did in the first forty seconds, so I said good-bye and moved on. I wonder if I was in too big of a hurry? Was I twenty seconds away from a surprise and now I'll never know? I knew I needed to mow the lawn and it was getting dark. I guess we can't second-guess ourselves all the time.

Lauren had a bunch of friends here when I got back from my ride—all hovering around the kitchen table. I love that. Our kitchen table is ground zero for everything of significance that happens at our house. I made a statement the other day saying that sometimes I think our kitchen table is more like church than, well, church. That's not a knock to our church or any other church, it's just that what happens here is real life, pretty much all of the time. You sit in a circle, eat food, look into each other's eyes, and talk about everything that matters. Sounds like church to me, or at least what church should be.

I read an article in the paper today that included a study that was done in 5,000 homes in Minnesota. It said that there was almost a 2 to 1 ratio of alcohol and drug abuse among kids whose families do not eat their meals together. I believe it. It might be the number one connecting time for our family. Scratch the "might," it is. We love it, and I know our kids do too.

I'd love to see more families worshiping at the Church of the Holy

Kitchen. We were doing this thing last year where every Wednesday night Taylor could invite any of her friends over for dinner. An open invitation of sorts. Sometimes there were two and sometimes a whole lot more. It got to the point where some kids just assumed they would eat with us on Wednesday nights. I loved that. So did Mary. So did the kids. But it kind of went away. Not sure why, but I think we need to bring it back.

That settles it; the Church of the Holy Fodder is back open. Or is it the Crystal Cuisine Cathedral? Temple of Chow Down? Maybe just Mother Mary's Soup Kitchen.

I hope our girls grow up with a love for kitchen conversation, and I hope they put the leaves in their tables so it becomes ground zero for their families — and friends.

Now it's dark outside — *midnight blue* dark. I fire up the Yardman and head out to buzz-cut my overgrown fescue. You know your life is getting out of hand when you're mowing the lawn during Letterman's monologue. It was kinda fun though — mowing by feel. In the morning I'll be able to see how good my "feel" was.

Looks like this will be the shortest entry in the journal so far. Sorry, you're just going to have to deal with it; I'm going to bed.

Oh, just remembered, last night at about 11:30, Lauren's friend, Jenny, asked if I could help them put air in her car tire. She thought it might be a little low. It was almost-touching-the-rim low! I took her and my daughter to the service station and gave them an "air-in-the-tire" lesson. They really didn't want a lesson. They just wanted air. Neither one of them wanted to get their hands dirty. Maybe we're like that with God. We just want him to keep us pumped up, but we don't really want to make the effort to unscrew the dirty, dusty cap. Do I want to get into this right now? I should really go to bed.

But I don't.

I'm sitting here, so tired and spent, and yet I just got the overwhelming impression that I absolutely love my life. It's so diverse, so interesting. I get to make music, write books, talk to people, ride my bike, sleep with my wife. Maybe I'm sleep deprived and delirium is setting in. If that's the case, bring it on. But I think it's more. It's a deep sense of having everything that I need to make my life complete. All that I need I already have. And all that I have is all that I need.

I feel very lucky. Maybe I should say blessed, but that word always feels weird to me, gives me the creeps. I've heard it misused and abused so often that I'm gun-shy to even mouth it. Well, I am blessed. There, I said it. Happy? Makes me feel that God really does love me.

I've thought about this a lot over the last few years — the sinking in of my belief in a God who loves me. It's easy to believe he loves other people, but it's not always so easy to believe that he's nuts about me. This is key. A primary understanding of life. I think that until we really, truly believe, from the bottom of our hearts, that God is crazy in love with us, we're living life as if in a tractor pull. Never getting anywhere, and the little progress we do make is a stinking lot of work. A joy killer. Who wants to spend a lifetime of spinning and tugging to go a hundred feet? No thanks.

God loves me. Sever the dead weight. God says, "Here, here are the keys to your soul, your Boxster. (I like to pretend that God thinks of me as his Porsche Boxster. I know, it's weird.) Go crazy. Test the limits of the talents I've given you. Push the envelope of your insecurities. Drop the hammer on your fear, pedal to the metal of your faith. Live large, live fast."

I think my joy is based in my growing belief that God thinks I'm a good thing. I'm *his* good thing. His invention, his Boxster. It would be a slap in his face if I didn't see how I corner. Every once in a while I need to test it out, see what I can do in a quarter mile. And use the brakes too, I suppose . . . if necessary.

You know how some people drive with their left foot on the brake all the time? That's living without the freedom that you are loved. Cautious. Fearful. Timid. Scared. Underachieving. So afraid of failure that success is sabotaged.

God don't let me live that way.

I'm going to bed. I've taken too many fast corners today. I'm hitting the brakes for about six hours. Hey, even Porches need to refuel. Zoom, zoom. Wait, that's Mazda.

Ignition off.

DAY NINETEEN: RAINING BOXSTERS

You know that stuff I was saying yesterday about knowing that you're loved by God and how that can totally change everything? Well, I kind of wrote that as an afterthought at midnight, but I don't want you to see it that way. I'm pretty sure that this might just be the most important thing I say in this whole thirty-day deal. Seriously. When you know you are loved by the Creator of the whole stinking universe, not much else matters. How could it?

That's it. Just wanted to reinforce it.

Today was a total wash. Spent twelve hours in the studio doing vocals and mixing on the Spirit FM radio station package. I worked with Mark and Scott. Good guys. Mark and three other guys own the studio together. I think I was the guinea pig, their first session. The studio has only been in operation for a week and a half. But, they did a great job. Scott, the engineer, is exceptionally fast, very efficient — I asked him if he was aware that he was getting paid by the hour. The studio, at gopher-level, reminded me of my early basement studio days. I spent countless hours underground in my early career. It works fine, but sooner or later you end up with yellow skin from lack of real light — studio jaundice. I grew to detest basements after a while.

Anyhow, Mark sang a few of the rock pieces while MJ sang bluesy and funk pieces. Then I had Stacy sing the pop/jazzy stuff. They all smoked it. Twelve hours into the day, I got the three main themes mixed, but then we just ran out of time. I headed for home, knowing that I was going

124

to have to send an e-mail to the station manager in Florida and explain that I had screwed up — I wasn't going to be able to deliver the job on time. The promised delivery date was today, and, well, today ran out. Bummer. I stopped on the way home and got an egg salad sandwich to-go and headed home to eat and watch a few minutes of the opening ceremony of the 2004 Summer Olympics. It was kinda fun. I plopped in a chair, the first moment in a long time where I just sat and vegged.

The ceremony was pretty low-tech, which surprised me. Impressive, but not the bells and whistles that I was expecting. I guess the Greeks don't feel the need to show off quite like we Americans do.

I sent a few of the music files via e-mail to the station with a stumbling explanation for my tardiness. Hope they understand.

Mary got home from work around nine. We haven't been seeing much of each other lately. I miss her when we miss each other. And we have been doing a lot of missing each other this month.

It was a long day. Don't know if I can point to any legit surprises today. Does that mean that God didn't answer my prayers today? Or was my agenda so predetermined and packed, wall-to-wall, that there was no space for him to be creative? I'm guessing God could choose to be creative and do a topsy-turvy thing with my day if he wanted to. Maybe he knew what I needed to accomplish and honored that. I guess he understands that I have responsibilities, that I need to generate income, that I've got mouths to feed, so he said, "Do your thing today and I'll just watch."

Days like this prevent me from sensory overload. Maybe he knows how much I can handle and he doles my surprises out in downloadable bytes. He knows my RAM, my CPU capacity.

Today was just routine, kind of blah, nothing out of the ordinary. It was one of those cloudy, nonstop drizzle days. No sun. A midnight blue day, I remember a poem I wrote a few years ago that kind of ties into this "dull day" idea. It's called Maybe Rain.

This poem is a dialogue between two guys. One who avoids the rain, the storm, almost afraid of it, and another guy who sees its potential. Maybe that's part of what this Surprise Me experiment is all about for me. Seeing potential in apparently potential-less days, potential-less conversations, even potential-less people.

Read it and see what you think.

Maybe Rain

By Terry Esau

What'a ya doin'?
Standing in the rain.
You're gonna get wet.
I know, I'm hoping to.
You could catch a cold.
Maybe.

Wanna borrow my umbrella?
No thanks.
Why not?
Then I wouldn't get wet.
You're crazy.
Maybe.

What's so great about getting wet?
What's so great about being dry?
Dry is comfortable.
Dry is safe.

Safe is good.
Maybe.

You like the danger of walking in storms?
Life _is_ a storm.
So you just walk straight through it?
If I wouldn't, it would walk through me.
You feel safe in the storm?
Maybe.

You know there could be lightning.
I know.
If it hit you, you'd be a goner.
Probably.
Aren't you scared?
Maybe.

Whoa! Did you hear that one?
Couldn't'a missed it.
It's getting closer.
I hope so . . . I think.
I suppose you're gonna stick it out?
Maybe.

What does it feel like, the storm?
Scary, thrilling, refreshing.
How do you know the storm will pass?
I don't, but it probably will.
Will you miss it when it's gone?
Maybe.

What would you think of me coming out there?

I think I'd like that.

Should I bring the umbrella?

If you want.

Do you think I need it?

Maybe.

This Surprise Me thing is like taking a walk in a storm. It's a quest for potential. It's an intentional wondering. Wondering how the rain will impact us even as we're stepping into it. Wondering what we'll find out there. Wondering who we'll find out there. It's stepping out of our comfort zone into the contact zone. It's stepping into the direct line-of-fire with life.

Where does the confidence come from to lean the umbrella up against the wall, push open the screen door, and walk confidently into the rain?

I think it comes from a deep understanding that the rain and the wind and the storm are gifts to us. Let me explain.

Remember yesterday when I was saying that maybe God looks at me like I'm a Porsche Boxster, his Boxster? And I said that it would be wrong not to put myself through the paces, test my cornering ability, handling, etc. Well, here's another question. Am I any less a Boxster when it's raining? Is a Porsche still a Porsche in the rain, or does it become something less?

Do dull days, dark days, painful days reduce our value? Do they make us less than we were? Does living life cause us to depreciate?

Of course not. On the contrary, I think we appreciate in value as we endure. Miles on our tread indicates wisdom. Rain beading up on our paint job indicates character.

Here's the question behind the question: does God love us *through* the rain or *with* the rain? If he only loves us through the rain, in the middle of the rain, then there would be no reason for us to step eagerly into the rain. Sure, we could be confident that he would be with us and encourage and sustain us in the rain. He could comfort us in the rain, but is that enough to make you want to chuck the umbrella and go puddle-jumping, all the while dodging lightning bolts? I don't know if I'm quite that masochistic.

But what if *we* believed he truly wanted to love us *with* the rain? What if the storm, itself, was a breed of love? And what if we will never really understand the totality of God's love for us until we walk out that screen door, sans umbrella, and look to the wind and rain for the intimacy it carries? Suppose "storm-love" is the deepest, most passionate expression of how he feels about us?

Automakers test cars in extreme conditions to find areas where they can improve them. Tires are matched against heat and water — do they hold, do they hydroplane? Suspensions are torqued, bumpers are crushed, SUVs are rolled. They don't do this to the cars because they hate them, they do it so the cars can realize their potential. It's a form of refinement. Mr. Porsche tortures his babies. Okay, "tortures" was not a good choice of words there, but that's probably how it feels to his Boxsters.

Here's the bottom line. As long as we understand who we are, God's high-tech, precision-designed, hand-crafted roadsters, we won't fear the rain, or the dull days, or the dark days, or even the painful days. I'm not saying we will enjoy them, although the Bible does say, "Consider it all joy when trials come your way." Never really liked that verse. But that statement right there shows what a revolutionary he is, Mr. Backward/Upside-Down Lover. Mr. Rain-Is-The-New-Sun dude.

Bottom-bottom line, "storm-love" is the sizzle and fizz of life. Chuck the umbrella. Potential-less is an oxymoron. Dull days, dark days, painful days might just be the greatest, most loving gifts our Creator can give us.

But I'm still not sure I like 'em.

DAY TWENTY: BRONCO BUSTING

Saturday morning—looking to be surprised.

I got up early today to write a speech. I'm speaking in a church tomorrow—fifty minutes worth. I know, I know, this too should have been done a long time ago. Life is surprisingly crazy these days. Surprisingly.

After a few hours of prep I decided I needed a break, so I took off on a bike ride by myself. I did the Navarre to Wayzata time trial. It's a 6-mile stretch snaking around the lake. About five years ago I set a goal for myself to break the 30-mph average for that stretch. The best I've gotten is 28.6 mph. So, I'm not even that close yet, and now that I'm fi, fif, fift—fi50fty (I have trouble with that word), I'm not sure it's going to be doable. But I haven't given up just yet. I'm waiting for the perfect day where there's a 50-mph tailwind out of the northeast that's just going to rocket me toward my goal. Stop snickering. Let me live my fantasy.

Today wasn't that day. I didn't even make a 26-mph average. I guess I was lacking commitment, energy, fitness, or all of the above.

Lauren, our middle daughter, heads back to Texas tomorrow, so we spent a good chunk of the day getting her packed up. Baylor University wants her back. Doesn't seem fair; I want her too. It just seems wrong that our kids grow up and then dump us for a college experience—not to mention that we have to pay dearly to get dumped. Where is the equity in that?

Packing makes me reminisce.

When Lauren was little she was a handful. If you looked up "feisty" in the dictionary, there was a mug shot of Lauren. Check it out; it's probably still there. She's sticking out her tongue, her eyes are crossed, and her fist is in the air. That's my baby.

She's gonna kill me for this, but when we were potty training her (or more accurately, when she was instructing *us* in how and when and where she would or wouldn't be potty trained), well, at one point she had "held it" in for almost forty hours. That's right; peristalsis was overruled for over a day and a half—a willful tapping of the tinkle.

We had refused to put a diaper on her, so she decided she would never pee again, just to spite us. For a while, we thought she might be able to pull it off. Hours into day two of the "*Urine Showdown*," her grandparents had taken our girls out to a hamburger joint for lunch. Maybe it was the first sip of the chocolate shake, or maybe just hearing the fountain machine running, but all of a sudden the dam burst. Now, we're not talking an amateurish little beaver dam here, we're talking the Hoover after a heavy rain. Remember President Reagan's trickle-down theory? Well, this wasn't that. They had to bring in a platoon of Wet Vacs. It was ankle-deep. Three inches past flood stage.

Yeah, it was an unsightly scene, but she never wore a diaper again. I tell you this to say that at times raising Lauren felt a bit like bronco busting. She could spit out a bit as fast as any filly I've ever seen. Well, at least in her younger years she did. As she got older, into her teens, something changed. She got softer, smarter, more logical. She chose her battles, and chose wisely. My fear of her splintering and kicking down every fence in sight to gain her freedom never materialized.

So now, as we're packing her up to leave, there's an odd sense that we're opening the gate for her to leave, willingly. Somehow, at this moment, her kicking the gate down seems to make more sense to me. I don't want to open the gate. No sooner does she get domesticated, tame—and we set her free? What's with that?

More packing.

I just remembered another Lauren story. I think this was about a year or two after the well-documented Hoover Dam Tinkle incident. We were driving by a cemetery one day and Lauren asked, "Why do people go camping after they die?" That's one of those questions it's hard to respond to because it feels so random and, uh, confusing. So I said, "Wwwwhat do you mean, camping?"

She explained how right after someone dies there's always a tent in the cemetery (you know, the canopy for the ceremony), so, obviously, that is the first order of business upon death. Camping.

Now there's an interesting twist on the streets of gold theory. Heaven as a celestial National Park, like Yellowstone, filled with RVs and Eurekas, Coleman lanterns, and down-filled sleeping bags. Jesus, the park ranger in goofy shorts, boots, and one of those funny hats. The four presidents on Mount Rushmore replaced with the Trinity — Father, Son, and Holy Ghost — carved into the side of Mt. Zion. Old Faithful spouting holy water, but it doesn't smell like sulfur anymore. That smell is reserved for a place south of the park.

The ranger will do programs at night in the amphitheater. Nature talks with a spiritual twist. Then we'll all gather around the campfire and sing cheesy songs like "Pass It On" and . . . wait a minute, we already do that here.

I wonder if there will be signs that say, "Don't feed the bears." I'm hoping we'll get to ride them. That would be cool — grizzly rides.

Mary sent me to the basement for another suitcase. Another weird daydream put to rest.

At dinnertime, we (my four girls — counting Mary — and I) headed to the North Coast, a restaurant on the shore of Lake Minnetonka. This was our big going-away dinner. We've done this every year, even before anyone was "going away."

When the girls were in their tween years, they didn't really like this tradition. They assumed it was going to be a "Come-to-Jesus" meeting, you know, where Mary and I would get on their cases and lay down the law with the new set of rules for the school year—curfew, chores, fun stuff like that.

Now that they're older, they know that this is a fun time. More of a looking ahead and dreaming than law-giving. Lately we've started a thing called the "five-year plan." It's a chance to go around the table and talk about where we see ourselves in five years. Brianna and Lauren did most of the talking here. Bri has just graduated from college and is doing a lot of thinking down the road. There's a guy in the picture too. She has big plans for him, I can tell. It's also pretty obvious that all of her plans include him. Pretty cool stuff, except I'm not sure how I feel about letting one of my fillies out, knowing she's not coming back, ever.

I don't want to talk about that anymore.

Lauren talked career choices, Taylor talked school and sports—they all talked boys. It's tough being me. All I've got are girls, and all they want to talk about is boys. I gave up and said, "Okay, tell me about what you like in a guy."

This was a fun discussion. It was interesting to see how what they like in a guy has changed over the years. Looks are still pretty high on the list, but not nearly the single factor it once was. There's a lot about sense of humor, personality, a "real" person—not someone who is always trying to impress or look good or compete or trash someone else or be all about themselves or cocky or arrogant or . . .

The list went on. There is never a shortage of words when we're talking about boys. Come to think of it, there's never a shortage of words at our house, period. It's a chatty world I live in.

The evening was fun and relaxing. We're so comfortable around each other that it is what it is. And I love what it is.

After dinner we went with Lauren to help her buy a digital camera to take to college. She's wanted one for a while and now we'll get pics online to keep up with her life. It's a good thing.

One more story about Lauren. This was a few years after the Hoover Dam Tinkle debacle and the Dawn of the Dead Campout. Mary's dad, Alf (yes, that's his real name, and no I didn't change it to protect the innocent—Alf is Alf, we love him, and to call him something else would just be wrong) was going in for open-heart surgery, quadruple bypass. It was a delicate time for all of us, but especially for our little girls. They were worried, and we weren't quite sure how to explain all that was going to happen. But we decided that the best approach was just to tell them exactly what it was and that we were confident that the good doctors would take care of their grandpa.

So we start to describe how the doctors would open his chest and make a path to Grandpa's heart and then—this is when Lauren's mouth fell open and she interrupted us. Her eyes got big and sparkly as she spit out the words, "Well, then the doctors will see Jesus!" It took us a moment to realize that all the talk of "Jesus in your heart" was more than metaphor to her. It was truth, literal truth.

It was a moment. A tender moment I will never forget. This headstrong bucking bronco of ours challenged and fought the reins in our hands, yet, she believed and trusted us implicitly on this one. There was a God who knew and loved her grandpa and lived inside of him. And that was that. Period.

The faith of a child, a colt. I'm a little jealous of that. This old steed is still only half-broken, still bucking. God, give me that kind of faith.

It's a cute story, isn't it? And you've got to admit, that would have been a surprise to end all surprises — if the doctors had gone in past the sternum and ribs only to find Jesus in goofy shorts, boots, and that little ranger hat. I imagine he would have cocked his head, looked at the doctors and said, "Tonight in the amphitheater we'll be talking about the marmot, a furry little critter that lives above the tree line in craggy rock outcroppings. And after that — grizzly rides!"

DAY TWENTY-ONE: STANDBY

I t's Sunday. I got up early to rehearse my talk. I walked Bailey and did the hurried "Surprise Me, God" prayer.

A lot of things have been hurried this month. I haven't spent much time reading the Bible during the experiment. At the beginning of this summer I bought a new paraphrase of the Bible called *The Message*. I "Amazoned" a copy with the intention of reading through it, cover-to-cover, by next summer. I think I'm through Genesis and that's about it. Two months, ninety pages. I guess we can make one deduction already about the Surprise Me thing — it's not dependent on proving to God that we're super-studious.

I actually like reading the Bible, sometimes. But it's not the only book I want to read when it comes to challenging myself spiritually. Some of you might not like that statement, and you may be right in feeling that way. But I get so much out of reading great authors talking about their life/spiritual journeys. If Jesus had come in 2004 instead of way back then, some of these contemporary authors may have been the writers of the Good Book. Who knows?

All I know is that I love being stimulated to think from a variety of sources.

Anyhow, where was I?

Brianna decided to come with me to my speaking engagement to help sell books afterward. It's a huge help because when people want to talk and books want to be signed, well, if I'm scrounging for change, things get backed up. I threw my guitar in the back of my old beater Beemer along with a few boxes of books, and we were off. Once there, I did a sound check while Bri set up the book table. Then we hung out and chatted with some people before the service started.

This was the first group I've "let in" on the Surprise Me thing. I explained the concept to them and then read the journal entry from July 27 — remember, the story about the biker guy? I considered picking one of the days where nothing of significance happened, but I didn't. I guess I wanted to impress them with how God did amazing things in my life. What does that say about me? I was even aware of that while I was reading. Weird, huh? What would they have done if I'd set up the scenario and then read them a dull story where nothing happened?

We sold a case and a half of books, met a guy who used to live across the street from me when I was a little kid, and got invited to someone's house for lunch. Bri and I declined the invitation because I needed to get home. Mary and I had to catch a plane in a couple of hours, headed for Texas — remember, we're moving Lauren into Baylor.

The flight was good, mainly because we got on it. I may have told you already, but Mary works for, well, one of the airlines, so we fly free . . . standby. Which is a fancy way of saying we are put in a position to get jerked around, with the outside chance of actually flying somewhere.

(Insert my mom's voice — "Terrance Gilbert Esau, you are so ungrateful.")

After all the paying passengers have boarded, the real game begins. It's like draft day in the NBA, except we don't have agents. Well, there's one agent — (Cue Beethoven's Fifth — duh, duh, duh, dum) — The Ticket Agent. Today it's Don King in a red vest without the humor and with twice the attitude.

All airline employees have been assigned a number that indicates their seniority, their worth to the team. Mary evidently isn't a franchise player. She's considered a "journeyman" role player. She's a 5F.

Now, I've seen her work, and let me tell you, she ain't no 5F. She should be a starter, the go-to person on the team, the "money girl," give her the rock! But I'm not the coach, er, ticket agent, so my take isn't worth diddly. We don't get called till round six, day two of the draft.

It's like when you were a kid and teams were being chosen for a game of driveway basketball. Everybody would line up for the Darwinian selection process. Stevie Larson was always the "unfit-est" to survive. I wonder if he was just happy to get picked, or if being last was worse than not being picked at all.

What if David Stern was God? If you wanted to play street ball in heaven you'd need a tryout. You'd need to pass a physical, have your blood drawn, furnish some impressive stats, do a 360-degree-behind-the-back-two-handed-slam-dunk with your eyes shut, have abs of steel, the Magic feel, be fleet of foot, ambidextrous, sport a marketable personality that would fill the stands and grow the brand, and be Yao-Duncan-KG-Stinking-Ming tall. Oh, and maybe an heir to Jordan. Basically, you would need to be more than you are.

If David Stern was God I think I'd be a 5F. There'd be a few billion people ahead of me in line. I'd be Stevie Larson, sweating it out.

Lucky for us, David Stern isn't God. We've all been offered a contract to be on his team. In 2 Peter 3:9 it says, "He is patient with you, not wanting anyone to perish, but everyone to come to repentance." The old *King James Version* says, "He is not willing that any should perish." *The Message* says, "He's giving everyone space and time to change." Maybe these thirty days are our "space and time."

Of course, there's that one sticky little detail—signing the contract. We don't make the team simply by receiving the contract, we've got to tender it, execute the copy committing ourselves to the team. How do we do that?

Here's where religion gets goofy. Lots of formulas have been created, prayers have been constructed, laws have been spiritualized, commandments memorized, faith categorized. A lot of theories have been thrown up and thrown down. Certain words and combinations of words have been canonized and come to signify the equivalent of a signature on the contract. "Pray this prayer, this way, and you're on the team."

I don't think it's that simple. Or maybe I should say I don't think it's that complicated. Here's what I do think, for what it's worth. I believe we sign the contract by falling in love with David Stern. I know that sounds weird, and I'll probably get a letter from him saying "What is wrong with you, boy?"

But, if God is this grand commissioner of humanity, and let's say Jesus is the coach, and for good measure let's make the Holy Spirit the trainer, well, then when we fall in love with the coach, the commissioner, and the trainer, and say, "Yeah, I really want to play for this team, I believe in this coach and this team and what they stand for, count me in." Voila, we're on the team.

It's really about knowing the commissioner, the coach, and the trainer, and then knowing us. However we get to that loving knowingness seems less important to me than arriving there. If your heart has arrived, then I suspect that the words that got you there were good. If you're in love with the God who made you, you're as good as picked. And I hope that by the time you're this far into the Surprise Me experiment, you're at least beginning to fall in love with this coach.

So, suit up teammate.

We arrived in Houston about 8 p.m., so obviously we got picked. I grabbed the courtesy phone in the airport for the car rental place and had an interesting conversation with Bernadette. She said, "Come on down and ask for me, Bernadette—remember, it's Bernadette. Burn—uh—det."

We got there and I walked up to an open agent and started taking care of things. All of a sudden a lady a few agents down asked, "Are you the guy on the phone?" I said, "Are you Burn — uh — det?" She said, "That's me and we're on commission here so step on down and get yourself in my line."

The agent I was working with slowly backed away from the counter. I observed a slight tremble in his hand. I looked at the guy and said very softly, "You're not afraid of Burnsie, are you?" He did an eyebrow thing, developed a throat-clearing tick, and slunk into the back room. I think she was the alpha male at Cheaper While You Wait Car Rental.

I wouldn't have messed with her either.

We drove to Waco on some way-back roads and got there around one o'clock in the morning. Lauren, who had flown down the night before, was waiting outside her apartment when we drove up. It was weird, like we were visiting her at her house. Our bronco had her own corral now. We went in, checked out the digs through bleary eyes, then took her with us to our hotel for the night. Lauren would have spent the night in 17D, but she didn't even have a mattress yet. That was tomorrow's task, along with a few dozen other things.

Finally got in and crashed like the Hindenburg. I fell asleep thinking about David Stern. Just before I drifted off, or right after, I'm not sure which, I was drafted as the new shooting guard for the Minnesota Timberwolves.

I guess that must have been after.

DAY TWENTY-TWO: MATTRESS SHOPPING

Morning came earlier than mornings have a right to. I got up first and showered, read a few words, checked my e-mail, prayed the prayer, and we were off.

The hotel offered a continental breakfast—a free continental breakfast.

Free.

Interesting word. I've never heard anybody say, "I got a free handful of dirt yesterday." Or, "I got a free piece of glass in my What-A-Burger." Or, "I got the flu last week—never paid a red-cent for it. Com-plete-ly free!" I guess free insinuates that the thing you get is something good, something you want.

Which brings me back to our free continental breakfast. Yyyeah. Enough said? Good. I can hear my mom again, "That's not a very grateful spirit, Terrance Gilbert." She's right. But I'm sticking with my views on free.

This was a fun and exhausting day. It was my task for this week to put Lauren's furniture together. I don't own a lot of power tools, and I don't know how to use them very well. Luckily, Lauren's boyfriend du jour does. Boyfriends are always eager to help. Makes them look good. And if they can help in front of the girl's dad . . . whoa, that racks up big points. I was just happy for the help and the tools. Do you realize how many screws come with a desk, a bed, a nightstand, a dresser, and . . . well you get the picture. And speaking of pictures, we pretty much performed

142

acupuncture on her walls. Posters, shelves, calendars. You really don't want any blank wall space to show, evidently.

We had shopped and paid for the furniture online. So all we had to do was show up and schlepp it to her apartment.

As we pulled into the parking lot of Pier One, my cell phone rang. It was NavPress, Terry Behimer, the editorial director. NavPress was one of the five publishers I sent this idea to. They were also the last and only one I hadn't heard from yet. Terry and I made small talk about moving a child into college and stuff like that for five or ten minutes. I kinda wanted to say, "Come on girl, what's the word? You like it or hate it?" But that would have been terribly uncouth, and authors have to act couth, whether they are or not. Usually, I figure if a publisher is calling me, they must have some interest, because rejecting something is so much easier to do in a form letter or e-mail.

Well, she was interested. Borderline excited. I sat in the car and gave Mary a signal that said, "this may take awhile" and she went in to expedite the furniture transaction.

Terry and I had a great talk. She really saw my vision for the whole Surprise Me thing. She understood it, and seemed almost as passionate about it as I was. Of course, I was okay with that. She told me that she and her husband had a Buddhist woman living with them for a while and was going to propose that they all do the "experiment" together and then talk about it at dinner at night. This is the very dream that I had had for this thing — people of varying and different faiths engaging together to find God in their everyday lives, and then talking about it together.

Before we hung up she said she was going to present it to the editorial board on Wednesday and then some other board after that. I didn't know they had so many boards to go through. I feel like I'm one of those karate dudes — I have to break three boards to get a contract.

Oh well, bring on the boards. I have an uncharacteristically calm confidence that this is the right idea for this time. It will land somewhere, somehow.

I finally flipped the lid on my cell and went in to tell Mary the news. She was a little too occupied with furniture to say much. For her, this trip was a focused event, a marathon of sorts. "We've got a room to decorate and make feel like home. Let's not get distracted here." I guess it's good. We balance each other out.

Tool-toting Tyler, the BDJ (boyfriend du jour), and I got the bed put together in an hour. His dad said it would take us three. Na, na, na-na, na! We da men! The desk took another hour, only because it was broken in a couple of spots. Otherwise, shoot, fifteen-twenty minutes, tops.

Mary and Lauren went to Target—the first of a dozen or so runs. I think I own stock in Target now, at the very least, I should. You name something, we bought it.

Next, mattress shopping—be still my heart. Now this was an education. I was amazed at all the choices, the subtle differences in these rectangular couriers of sleep. You got your coil springs. You got your Futons. You got your air mattresses, your feather beds, your Serta, your Simmons, and your Sleep Number. You got your King Koil and your Coil King. You got your high-tech, space-foam, body-molding Posturpedic with plush pillow-topped, posture-zoned, double-tempered innersprings with hypo-allergenic conjugated fibers, No-Flip technology, stress-relieved, heat-tempered individually pocketed 15-guage coils to assure a firm Total Torsion system with a Motion Separation Index of 184, gasp, all with a 10-year warranty.

Exhale.

Mattresses are a lot like religious denominations—you can't tell them apart till you lay down on them. Even then, they're kind of subtle. And once you fall asleep, the differences tend to become inconsequential because, well, you're sleeping and you're oblivious to their differences. And the point, really, is to sleep, not to stay awake pointlessly analyzing the mattress.

The purpose of the mattress is to be a vehicle of sleep.

Let me repeat that.

The purpose of the mattress is to be a vehicle of sleep.

When religious denominations become more than a vehicle to God, they're nothing but lumpy mattresses with arrogant, imprudent springs. If your mattress has excessive stuffing that keeps you awake at night, maybe God's not in it. You're better off sleeping on the ground. It might be hard, but it's true.

This really isn't a critique of denominations; it's more of an indictment against we-the-people who make up the denominations. And that includes me. We're the ones who tend to make it more than simply a vehicle to God. We're the ones who stuff the mattress with fluff, usually to make ourselves look better, or to show that we're right, or to prove that whoever isn't with us is wrong. In the meantime, people lose sleep because there are a lot of us self-righteous springs in these lumpy mattresses. God, don't let me be that spring anymore.

Next.

Lunch at Fazoli's. Then we went over to the BDJ's apartment to see how he lives. His apartment is in a converted furniture factory. It's pretty funky—looks like a cross between a prison and a loft. Who knew the prison look would become hip? Pretty soon we'll all be wearing orange jumpsuits.

Where are the surprises in this day? I guess when I woke up this morning I wasn't imagining the tie between my Happy Sleeper and the Baptist General Conference. Surprise.

One last thing. You know that whole litany about the mattresses? Well, the foundation, the bed supporting the mattress is God. We wander through life tired, exhausted, looking for something to lay our head on that's real, true, and honest. We're looking for a peace that knows what love is. When God sees a human who loves him and trusts him enough to fall asleep in his arms, I have a hard time believing that he cares whether the springs were sprinkled or dunked.

What matters to him is that our love led us to trust — to lay ourselves at his feet in submission and surrender. The bed has done the work. The mattress is the vehicle. We are the beneficiaries. It might not hurt us to sleep around on a few other mattresses and find that God's people sleep there too.

All this sleep-talk is making me . . . sleepy. I think I'll set my Motel 6's Sleep Number bed to 65 and catch a few . . . yeah, right. No sleep number here.

I wonder if I'll even be able to fall aslee . . .

DAY TWENTY-THREE: NO TV?

Tuesday morning came even earlier than Monday morning—and Monday morning was rooster happy. This is the time of day I like to be examining the inside of my eyelids, admiring the midnight blue hue, but evidently we had stuff to do.

Ah, the venerable "stuff."

Yesterday was big-item assembly; today is minutiae management. Wall hangings, pictures, curtains, lights, shelves, bedding, necessity shopping, book shopping, computer setup, etc. Again today I had the able hands of BDJ—the boyfriend du jour. I suppose if a BDJ remains constant and in the picture for a series of consecutive weeks and months, at some point I'm going to have to call him something else—like RD'05 or SSB (Somewhat Serious Boyfriend) or LTB (Long-Term Boyfriend). I know, Triple B—Bucking Bronco's Boyfriend. Yeah, I like the ring of that. We'll see how Lauren feels about it.

Anyhow Triple B, Mary, me, and the Bronc were busy little beavers. We spanked that bedroom into a state of cozy that would have made those Queer Eye guys jealous. There were many times during the day when we just backed into the doorway and admired our handiwork. Considering that Triple B and I are straight, we're dangerously good at décor.

After a few hours of making her room fun, we went to the bookstore to get Lauren's books for the fall semester. We bought used.

We looked for books that didn't have excessive underlining or highlighting in them. Lauren doesn't like excessive highlighting that didn't come from her pen. I understand that. It feels like you're reading along and all of a sudden a phrase screams at you and you say, "What? Why are you yelling? That phrase means nothing," I know how she feels. We found books with minimal yellow yelling.

After lunch, Lauren went to training for a freshman orientation thing, so we had time to kill.

What better way to kill time than shopping for knick-knacks? Lauren needed important things like a toothbrush holder so we went to a place called Spice. I start twitching at the very sight of knick-knacks, so I sat outside on a bench and read the new David Sedaris book, *Dress Your Family in Corduroy and Denim.*

One of the chapters was called Us and Them. It talked about a family that moved into a neighborhood . . . and didn't have a television. It's not that they didn't believe in TV, they just didn't have one. Well, that got the neighbors talking about all kinds of bizarre reasons for the lack of TV. It snowballed to the point where they avoided each other because they didn't think they'd be able to relate to one another. How could you understand somebody who didn't even have a TV? They were just too different. And different was bad.

Sound familiar? It reminds me of the "Us vs. Them" mentality that saturates our culture. Urban vs. rural, red states vs. blue states, skaters vs. jocks, men vs. women, white vs. black, right vs. left, gay vs. straight, conservatives vs. liberals, Christians vs. non-Christians. When one of these groups moves into our neighborhood, we peek in their windows and see that they don't have a TV. We start talking. We profile Them. We make assumptions. Then we project those assumptions on everyone who wears the same label. We generalize. We focus on our differences. And as everybody knows, differences are bad!

The Us vs. Them thing especially bugs me when it comes to Us, we the Christians. When we start looking at non-Christians as Them, we might as well pull the gun out of the holster and shoot ourselves in the foot. In fact, we might as well empty the clip into our foot.

First we see that they don't go to church, or at least not our church. Assumption — they don't know the Truth. Then we find that they vote differently than we do. Assumption — they're destroying the fabric of our country. Then we catch them drinking a little too much or saying some words that make us uncomfortable. Assumption — we need to get them out of our neighborhood; they're evil.

Don't hear me wrong, I'm not saying we should condone drunkenness or immoral behavior of any kind, but have we looked in a mirror lately? Are we poster children for the moral law? Can we honestly say, "Yes, I could throw the first stone. Gimme a big one!"

All I'm saying is that before we know it we've moved from curious to bothered to irked to irritated to mobilized to militant to contempt to hatred. Now we've made Them the enemy.

And all this started because they didn't have TVs?

Remember, at one point we didn't have a TV either. Then one day we decided to go shopping at Best Buy and pick one up. Turns out, they had a weird sale going on. Some philanthropist dude had purchased the entire inventory of TVs and was offering them for free. You just stop in and pick one up. The price was paid, bingo, we had a TV. In an almost undetectable moment we went from TV-less to TV-yes. TV-Hell to TV-Heaven.

From Them to Us.

You realize, of course, that non-Christians can go out and get a TV anytime they want. I mean, the price has already been paid; their TV has already been bought. They just haven't picked it up yet. So they too could become Us at any moment. Doesn't it track then, that we should treat Them as merely future Us-es? They're just a shopping trip away from joining our team.

Why do we do battle with the very people who will likely be standing beside us? What's this eagerness to defend and protest and confront? Wouldn't it be better to invite these neighbors over to watch our TV? Perhaps they'd say, "Wow, I like the TV. The TV's cool. Maybe I should get one for myself." And we could say, "They've got a great deal on them at Best Buy. It's already paid for. All you've got to do is go pick it up."

This wide-screen picture of faith sort of repaints that whole "TV will rot your brain" thing, doesn't it?

Lauren got out of her orientation thing early, around three in the afternoon. So we had time for another Target run. We bought an iced tea maker. Iced tea is a tasty bad habit in our family. I think some guy in a back alley forced Mary to try it intravenously. She became an addict and then graduated from junkie to dealer providing the family with our black market/black current fix ever since. Now our poor Lauren is all strung out on tea. It's sad what happens when parents can't control their addictions.

We went to Ninfas, a great little Mexican restaurant, for dinner and then took Lauren and Triple B out for custard ice cream. We spent the evening sitting around, talking, and admiring Lauren's new apartment. Enchiladas, refried beans, and custard ice cream tend to slow the metabolism to a point where sitting seems like all the activity you can handle.

Well, that was the day. How did it look on the Surprise-o-meter? Did you see any? Sometimes I wonder if I need to rethink my definition of surprise. Or maybe I should have called this experiment Teach Me. Or Confuse Me. Or Make Me Go Off On Weird Metaphorical Tangents For No Apparent Reason. Hmm . . . that would be an interesting book title. Nah. But I'm sure you've noticed by this point in the book—I gravitate toward metaphors. It's like metaphors have formed a giant black hole in my head and I can't help but be sucked in every time I sit down at the computer to write.

See what I mean?

I think when I get back to the hotel tonight I'll watch some TV. Maybe I'll invite my neighbors over to watch too. I wonder if they have one of their own?

DAY TWENTY-FOUR: WINDOW SHOPPING

This was it, our last hours with Lauren before heading back to Minneapolis. So how did we spend it? Eating breakfast at Cracker Barrel. Fruit pancakes. Bacon, eggs, English muffins and jam—and iced tea. I know, iced tea is not really a breakfast drink, but we're addicted. Remember? On the way out, an older man saw that Lauren was carrying an *In Style* magazine. He looked at her and asked, "Why are you looking at that? You're prettier than the girls in there." I wasn't sure if I should punch him out or say, "I couldn't agree with you more."

Before we left Cracker Barrel, I visited the restroom. While, uh, there, I heard a song come over the intercom. An old traditional country-and-western song that I assume was called Window Shopping. The chorus went like this:

> *You're just window shopping*
> *Window shopping*
> *You're only looking around*
> *You're not buying*
> *You're just trying*
> *Looking for the best deal in town*

This was a serious twang-a-lang song—the steel guitar was crying, the bass was weeping, and the singer was crooning. I almost got teary-eyed. Of course, that was because of all the shopping we'd done in the last forty-eight hours, and none of it was window shopping. It was the real deal, credit card swiping and all.

All through the day today I couldn't get that ridiculous song out of my head. It made me wonder if I was supposed to be culling something from those deep lyrics.

We had a couple of hours to kill before heading back to the airport, so we took a tour of the new science building. In the atrium is the Java City coffee shop, where Lauren will be working, part-time, this fall.

I wonder if NavPress has had it's editorial meeting yet?

Our last order of biz before leaving Waco was to drop in on Greg, an English professor at Baylor. Terry Behimer told me about him. He has a book coming out on the NavPress label this fall. She sent twin e-mails to Greg and me, introducing us, virtually. She fed us each other's numbers and info, so I called him and set up a short meeting.

Now get this, and you tell me if this is coincidence or Surprise Me-incidence.

I'm nuts about cycling—Greg has written a novel called Cycling. He's a music guy/guitar player turned writer—me too. I'm reading through The Message—Greg and a few other guys have been contracted to write a more artsy, younger targeted version of The Message, the Bible. He's writing it with Donald Miller and a couple other guys, who, it just so happens, have written the very books I've been reading the last few months.

Does God place these people in our lives for us to connect with? People who "get" who we are? People who have a role to play on this path of ours, even if we haven't discovered where it goes? When are circumstances divine and when are they not? And should we even try to decipher between the two?

Coincidence or Surprise Me-incidence? I don't know.

Back to Greg. He was so kind, offering to help Lauren in any way

153

he could. He said he'd be happy to talk to her about anything during the school year. You gotta love profs like that. Maybe he can be a father-in-residence in my absence.

We dropped Lauren back at her apartment and said good-bye. I gave and received a hug that would need to hold me for several months. Have you ever noticed how the tightness of a hug is proportional to how long it will be before you get to do it again? It was hard to leave her. A block later I already missed her.

On the way back to Houston, we drove through the metropolis of Mart, Texas. Literally hundreds of people live there. Mary's father knows the father of the woman who is the postmaster in Mart, so he said, "If you ever go through Mart, you've got to stop and say hi to . . ." uh, whatever the lady's name is who is the postmaster there. Neither of us knew her name, nor did we have a clue where the post office was. And I didn't care. I know, that's a stinky attitude, but we needed to get to the airport. So, as we're approaching Mart, Mary looks over at me and says, "It would mean a lot to my dad if we stopped in at the post office and said hi to, uh, whatever the lady's name is who is the postmaster there."

Pause.

I guess I must have given her a condescending look of disbelief. And I might have said something like, "I don't think so." Which in retrospect probably weren't the ideal words for that exact moment. As we entered the "city" limits, I could feel a couple of eyes on me — no words, just eyes. I hate that. You know how you pretend you don't notice it for a while, and then it just drives you nuts so you whip your head to the right and irritably say, "What?!" [Rules of punctuation broken intentionally — I call it a "questlamation mark."]

A little more silence. Then two words.

"You're selfish."

Oh, them's fightin' words. How dare she accuse me of being selfish?

I just blew four days off work. I just put together a bed, a desk, drawers, racks, and a bunch of other stuff that I didn't really want to put together. I just heated my credit card up to a near liquid state by excessive swipe-o-holism. I endured knick-knack shopping, for Pete's sake, toiletry arranging, closet organizing, curtain hanging, apartment decorating, and, and . . . she's calling me selfish? Well, I never . . .

I blurted out, "So just because I won't stop in to visit someone I've never met, never heard of, never really wanted to meet, in a town in the middle of nowhere, who happens to be the postmaster and the daughter of a guy who just happens to know your dad — I'm selfish?"

"Yup."

Breathe. Deep breaths.

All I could come out with was, "Well, I have no idea where the post office is so . . ." At that very moment I saw the post office about thirty yards in front of us. Great. Now what do I do? I whipped the car into an open spot, threw it into park and said, "We're here."

We went in to meet good old what's-her-name.

She wasn't there.

Mary wrote a note explaining how and why we had stopped in and who we were and how we wished we could have met her. Then we left. Got in the car and drove away — in silence. In twenty miles it was over and we were laughing again, kinda — sorta. Then Mary fell asleep and left me with my thoughts and processing the S-word, and how it related to me.

Here's the deal, I don't like being called selfish, but I am. I know it, Mary knows it, most of my friends know it. It's not breaking news to God. The funny thing is, that of all these people, I think I was the last one to come to the realization I was selfish. It wasn't until we had children that I discovered it at all.

When we have kids, they become like mirrors. They allow us to see ourselves as we really are. They push all of our buttons, all at once sometimes. Sooner or later the real me shows it's ugly self. It happened and I saw a big "S" on my forehead.

Here's the truth about me. I like my own way, I think I'm right, and if you don't agree with me, there's a really good chance that I think you're wrong. So, maybe it's not just selfishness, maybe there's some arrogance sprinkled in there too. Ouch.

Oh, and by the way, I'm still in denial about it. Much of the time. I still think I'm usually right. Is that just the human condition, or is it me? Am I just that screwed up? Well, today I saw it again, my selfishness. If I wouldn't have come across that post office, I don't think I would have looked for it. I wouldn't have stopped and politely asked, "Where can a guy who doesn't have a dang thing to mail find a stinking post office in this God-forsaken town?" (My apologies to the entire population of Mart, TX. I'm sure God really hasn't forsaken you. Maybe I should say Terry-forsaken town. Then apologize for that, too.)

But we did come across it, right in front of us, right as I said I would never find it. Is that a Surprise Me-incidence? I think the surprise had very little to do with the post office, or the postmaster, or any of that. I think the surprise for me today was seeing my selfishness. To see myself, as I am. I can be a real jerk.

We finally made it to Houston and dropped off the car. I told the car rental attendant that the tank wasn't full when we picked it up; in fact we had a note from the checkout person when we drove away with the car saying that the tank wasn't full. He said we'd have to go to the main desk to tell them. As I rounded the corner, there was Bernadette, the checkout clerk with the bad-itude from a few days earlier. I paused and realized I didn't need three bucks that badly. We headed for the shuttle.

We killed time at the airport watching the Olympics while munching nachos con queso at Chili's. That Michael Phelps is a freakin' fish.

Sitting on the plane, I kept wondering how the NavPress editorial meeting had gone today. I wondered why they hadn't called.

Wheels up—wheels down. Bri picked us up from the airport. It's a cool thing—we hugged a daughter good-bye on one end of the flight, but we got to hug another one hello on this end. There is justice in the world after all. We told stories all the way home.

Bailey was happy to see us. You gotta love dogs.

Taylor was gone, partying; the girl has a life. Before long the party ran out so she came home and we snuggled.

That's day twenty-four. As Mary and I fell into the end of the day, our bed felt good. I fell asleep hoping for pleasant dreams . . . and praying they wouldn't morph into nightmares featuring the entire population of Mart, Texas, knocking down my door, Night of the Living Dead-style.

I'm sure I'd really like them all. Honest, I would. Especially whatever the lady's name is who is the postmaster there.

DAY TWENTY-FIVE:
COUNTING SURPRISES

6:30 a.m. After flying in late last night, an early morning recording session is not exactly what I was hoping for. But I've already had to beg off for being a week behind on delivery of this package, so 6:30 it is.

I prayed the Surprise Me, God prayer on the way to the session as I picked up an Egg McMuffin. When I got to the studio, I found out that my engineer had been mixing since 5:30 a.m. to help me get a jump on things. I owe him. That's surprise number one today.

We plowed through the mixes, painlessly. I was interrupted multiple times during the session with phone calls. Normally I would shut down my cell, but I knew I had some interesting calls coming in today, so I stayed powered up.

The first was from my daughter, Bri. She had interviewed for a job at a local school district. I had asked her to let me know how it went. "Good," she said. For a girl that can rival many authors with colorful verbiage, "good" didn't tell me much. Maybe she was just being safe, you know, trying not to get her hopes up.

A few minutes later the phone rang again. It was the promotions director for a TV station in Maine. They wanted to know how much it would cost them to license a music package I had done for a local TV station. Passive income—always a good thing. Surprise number two?

I think I'll try counting my surprises today. See what happens.

One ID mix later my pocket jangled again. It was NavPress, Terry

158

Behimer. She said the meeting with the editorial staff went great (Surprise #3). She said they wanted to make me an offer, but then pulled back, saying that she couldn't officially do that until the whole board got to look at it. However, they pushed the meeting up to next Tuesday. Earlier she had said that wouldn't happen for two weeks. They seem eager to move on this thing. I like that. I need to decide how to handle the other two publishers who have expressed interest. Obviously, I need to talk to them and see what they are thinking. I guess it's a good position to be in.

Finished the session. Tipped the engineer.

I called Mary on the way home from the studio and asked her to meet me for lunch at D'Amico. We ran into some of Lauren's old basketball buddies and their moms. It was fun; we talked and reminisced. They asked how Lauren was doing and told us to say hi to her. They wished me a happy birthday, which had happened a month earlier (Surprise #4). Mary had thrown me a huge party because it was one of those "significant" birthdays (let's just say I've been AARP-ed). Anyhow, they had missed the big soirée and were now taking advantage, ribbing me on my advanced age.

After lunch I came home and packaged up the CDs for Spirit FM. I FedEx-ed them to Florida. Job done. Feels good.

I decided to reward myself with a bike ride. I met Gary out on the road; he had already put in forty miles by the time I met up with him. We cruised. It's been almost a week since my last ride and my stubbed toe didn't scream at me like it did then. Gary and I did the Navarre to Wayzata time trial — and I crossed the "finish line" with a 26-mph average. Again. Wouldn't it have been nice to include a 30-mph record-breaking achievement as part of this Surprise Me collection? I guess, but not getting it just reminds me that God isn't my genie. When I need something (read: want something) I can't just buff his lamp and out he pops to grant my every wish — regardless of how trivial or self-serving it is. Still, I like to fantasize. ESPN leads with the story, "Terry Esau, late entry in the Tour de France, wins by shellacking Armstrong. Oldest man ever to win Tour" (Surprise #5 — wait, that doesn't count, I was just imagining it.)

What if God was that easy? What if we could manipulate him? Scary. If God was my tool, instead of me being his, I'm afraid a lot of things would get broken, besides records. I'd probably swing him like a hammer to get my way. There'd be a few people with egg-shaped bonk marks on their heads. Yeah, it's a good thing God's not my tool.

Came home and mowed the lawn and then leaf-blew the driveway. Have I told you about my leaf blower? This thing is cool. You strap it on your back and if you point it straight down at full throttle you can almost achieve liftoff. I swear I could do damage to mobile home parks with it.

Tonight it was dinner out with Mary at Chez Foley. (I've noticed something from keeping this journal; we eat out a lot during the summer. Maybe that's a surprise I'm supposed to see (Surprise #5 — really.). We throw too much money at French and Italian restaurateurs (and Mexican, and Thai, and Chinese, and Indian, and . . .) While there, Mary ran into a high school girl whose mom had suddenly died. Mary was able to check in and see how she was doing and encourage her.

This is a very cool thing about my wife. First of all, she remembers everyone, and I mean everyone. How does she do that? And she remembers their stories, what's happening in their lives. She asks lots of questions, not out of nosiness, but out of care and love. And then she listens.

I could learn from that. I should have learned from that already. She's modeled it for years. People are what matters to Mary. She understands that whole "love your neighbor as yourself" thing pretty well.

Sometimes I think I have too much of a personal agenda spinning around in my head. So when I run into people, it's not always my first thought to see how they are, what's new with them, or how I can encourage them — sometimes it's too much about me. I tell them about my new project, my latest scheme. Did I say scheme? I meant dream. I think (Surprise #6).

And speaking of schemes and dreams, sometimes, in my most honest moments, I wonder if this Surprise Me thing is partly about me. I suspect it is. I rarely have 100 percent pure motives with anything, why would this be any different? It's a good thing that this is just my own personal diary; nobody's going to read it. I'm disclosing a little too much information for this thing to go public.

Ooops (Surprise #7).

I wonder if some of my friends, after they read this, will come up to me and say, "I didn't know you were such a twit." I wonder if they'll come up to my kids and say, "Your dad's weird. I feel sorry for you." Maybe I *should* rethink this.

Oh, today was the day they named the varsity roster for soccer. She made it. Our little Tator Tot made varsity. I think I was more excited than she was. Some of her good friends didn't make varsity, so it was a bit awkward for her. It's hard to show too much exuberance when making the team if your friends are feeling down about missing out. Tay's not a gloater, so I'm sure she was smug-free and sensitive. She takes after her mother. Thank God.

I checked the news before bed tonight and saw that Tyler Hamilton won gold today in the cycling time trial at the Olympics (Surprise #8). This guy is my hero. Last year he was racing in the Tour de France, and on the first stage he was involved in a pile-up crash and broke his collarbone in two places. Many of us were thinking he would be the biggest competition for Lance Armstrong. But suddenly he was out.

Not so fast. He got up the next morning and asked the doctors what risks he would be taking if he tried to ride. They looked at him funny and proceeded to tape his shoulder together as tightly as they could. He rode that day. He rode the next day. He grimaced on the early climbs. He was gritting and grinding his teeth so hard from the pain that he actually had to have many of them recapped after the 'Tour.

Well, this guy not only won stage eighteen of the Tour on a solo breakaway, but he ended up taking fourth overall. This is unbelievable. Do you realize how much pushing and pulling with your arms is necessary in bike racing?

So today, to see him weaving and gasping at the end of the Olympic Time Trial, giving every last ounce of his soul to win the gold, well, it's just flat out inspiring. Here's to you Tyler. You're Surprise #8 today.

I guess eight surprises in one day is good. If I fall asleep within one minute, I'll count that as number nine. Tomorrow, I'm going for ten.

But then, they're not up to me, are they?

DAY TWENTY-SIX: STEPFORD CHRISTIANS

My first meeting today was at Starbucks with Greg, the associate pastor at our church. We talked about Surprise Me for two hours. Greg was originally in the music biz like me, so we got sidetracked for a while and talked studio gear — digital audio workstations and plug-ins. There are still days I miss The Coast, my studio, and the excitement of assembling a group of killer musicians and hearing them play something I've written. But like I said, a guy can only sell so much kitty litter before his soul begins to smell like a litter box.

On the way home from Starbucks I got a call from Steve, one of my old college roommates. I told him about the Surprise Me idea. He liked it. My college roomies, Steve, Dutch, and Dan are always good sounding boards. The four of us get together for lunch about once every other month. We always meet at Fuddruckers. Yeah, yeah, we're classy dudes, I know. We've tried other, cooler, hipper places but we always come back to Fudds, because that's where we started meeting years ago, and the history of the conversations we've had there just seem to draw us back.

I wish I could record one of our Fudd sessions and play it for all of you. It zigs from family to God to movies to sex to career, then zags from theology to anger to selfishness to Grand Funk Railroad to confession to, well, anywhere — everywhere. Nothing is sacred with us. Or, more accurately, everything is sacred. All I know is that our discussions verge on the brutally honest, every single time we're together. We hold mirrors up to each other and challenge each other's thinking and behavior. But

163

the cool thing is, I've never, not even once, left these guys feeling like they've judged me. We all know way too much about each other to ever consider throwing a stone. Besides, none of us has any desire to throw a stone. I love those guys. I wish you all knew them like I do.

After lunch I went for a bike ride with Grant. He's nineteen, in college now, but was part of the high school small group I led for the last few years. He sends me e-mail updates of his life every once in a while that are pretty entertaining. Here are a few sentences:

I started my sweet job after about a week and soon learned that I actually do get paid to sit in a golf cart and watch freshmen girl's soccer, placing a check on a sheet of paper when someone scores. It is by far the best job I have ever had. I get my own golf cart, 'honestly.' I have been to every girl's soccer game so far and am pleased to say that I and 5 of my good buddies will be ball girls at the 1:00 p.m. game vs. UTEP. Why, you might ask? I'll tell you why; we get small T-shirts that say "Rice Soccer — Official Ball Girl" Why on earth not! Oh and the girls on the team are really cute.

Grant, Grant, Grant. Who would have guessed such a fine outstanding young man with so much potential would grow up to be a ball girl? Was it my influence?

Grant's dad, Tom, was also on the bike ride with us. I wonder if he knows about his son's "aspirations." Anyhow, Tom and I are talking about doing a biking trip to France next year. Tom says he's going to lose twenty pounds before the trip and then gain every one of them back by gorging himself everyday on that fabulous French food. Sounds like a good plan to me.

Lauren called this afternoon. She's leading a freshman orientation group, and last night, one of the new girls didn't show up. They found out later she had been involved in a terrible car accident on the way to Baylor and was killed. Lauren was pretty shaken by this. Isn't it bizarre how one second everything is going great, you're on your way to the next stage of your life, college, and then everything changes?

I'm tempted to get into a discussion here about those kind of surprises. You know, the bad ones. What if this student had been in the middle of a Surprise Me experiment of her own? What if her dad was? What if I was her dad, and on that morning I had awakened and prayed, "God, surprise me." How would I deal with that? I don't think I can even answer that, and I hope to God I never have to wrestle with it. I feel for her family.

Lauren said it was weird to think that they are going to be making fajitas together tonight, and this girl, who had been planning on that too, won't be there. It's hard to understand.

Mary and I went to Monkabeans for dinner. It's this one-off, quirky coffee shop with garage-sale furniture and no discernable color scheme. Where would we be without funky little coffee shops? I love 'em.

After Monkabeans, Mary and I went to see *The Stepford Wives*, the remake version. It was at the two-dollar theater. I felt like I was watching a movie about faith. Seeing all those 36-24-36, cookie-cutter cuties — with their porcelain smiles stuck in the on position — well, for a second I thought I was in church. It was the charge of the religious lemmings. All those pristine, plaster-of-Paris wives reminded me of a whole satellite dish-full of TV Christians I've seen. And a bunch who aren't on TV. Yes, I saw myself in them too. That was the scariest moment in the movie — seeing myself as a Stepford Christian.

I suppose being a robot Christian might be easier — very little thinking involved. I know I have fallen into that brain-dead mold more often than I'd like to admit. But you gotta wonder, is that what God had in mind? When Nicole Kidman kissed Matthew Broderick in the movie, she was real, he could feel her skin, smell her breath, and taste her lips. He knew she was organic. Robots don't give good feel. She made a sales pitch with that kiss. "What you just kissed wasn't no robot, baby," she said. "That wasn't artificial, coerced, programmed love."

When Jesus willingly accepted our kiss of death, he wasn't saying, "Fake like you love me, people. Be my robot. As long as you look good on the outside, then my death will have all been worth while." He didn't take the nails for robots. He did it for skin-covered humans with minds saturated in free will. He did that because he knew he could handle our organic-ness. He knew he could handle our questions. He wanted us to question, because only nonrobotic living beings question. Only cell-wrapped hearts could love reciprocally, with a tangible love that God could feel, smell, and taste.

That's why it is so pathetically sad that we Christians have become robotic in this culture. I'm pointing the finger at me too. We act, we play roles — a part we've read about, a part we've been told we're supposed to play. We're ceramic plaster-of-poser. We may look good to the casual observer, but what good is the casual observance when you're looking for ultimate substance? As long as we are just role-playing, the only participants we're going to bring on board are other role-playing, bit-part thespians who are looking for nonthinking parts. We've got enough nonthinkers in Christianity. We need genuine, questioning wrestlers of the faith. We need people who doubt their way to belief. People who question their way into ownership of their faith. People who earn the right to say, this is who I am, so far, because this is who I've discovered God to be, so far. Donald Miller, in his book *Blue Like Jazz* (which you should all go out and buy and read) said he likes God because God doesn't resolve. What? You're admitting that God confuses you — that you can't always figure him out?

That's not the voice of a robot. Good!

We have too many Christian robots. We need Christians who fail and admit they fail. We need Christians who admit that they don't know everything. We need more human Christians. We need more Christian humans.

Let's wrestle our beliefs to the ground. Then let's get up and do it all over again. Let's be okay with the struggle, with not knowing everything.

Do we really want a God that we can explain? Do we want a God that we can quantify? If we could, wouldn't we be him? I don't want that God. If I can figure him out, then I don't want him. He'd be too average, too regular, too human. That God's a poser. The robots can have that God. He's not worthy of my devotion. I want a big God that blows my mind into tiny bits when I even attempt to capture him.

I want a God who's a surprise machine, a conundrum, a continual mystery.

That's the God that has captured me. I know for a fact that he doesn't resolve, at least in the way that I understand resolution. And I'm becoming more and more okay with that. I'd better, because there are no other options.

Whew. That felt kinda good. Doesn't it seem that every time we miniaturize God, instead of making us look bigger, which is what we naturally want to do, by the way, it just makes us small and stupid? The bigger our God is, the bigger we become. The more real and honest our God is, the more real and honest we become. The more loving our God is, the more loving we become.

God, I'm glad you're not Stepford. Reduce the Stepford in me.

Okay, all this deep thinking has made me tired. I'm going to go lay my partially porcelain head on my pillow.

DAY TWENTY-SEVEN: ALL OR NOTHING

The "beautiful game" starts again today for Taylor. It was a stunningly perfect Saturday morning. A great day for a soccer scrimmage — the first of many for my varsity squad daughter. It started out cool, around 50, but the sun burned off the fog and warmed us up on the sidelines.

"Surprise Me, God."

It was about a forty-mile drive to where the games were played today, and Keith and I drove together, stopping for breakfast along the way. Mary had to work.

We ate at the Countryside Café, which is one of those down-home little joints where it looks like you stepped into an old cabin. It was packed. The servers in those places are always older women who chew gum and say, "What'll ya have, honey?" They never look happy, but you suspect they are. Their names are always Flo or Marge.

We had one of those servers; however, in the Countryside Café I suspect they're still called waitresses. I had raspberry French toast, which seems wrong for a place like this, but it was pretty tasty.

The walls were plastered with pictures of people who come to the Café. Keith and I wondered if someone was going to come by and Polaroid us. No one did. Maybe you have to be a regular to get snapped and tacked to the wall. I'm not sure if my cholesterol can handle becoming a regular.

I wonder if walking into a church for the first time is a bit like walking into the Countryside Café? Everybody else looks like regulars; they all have their pictures on the wall. They all have a regular seat. They all look suspiciously like Flo or Marge, not too happy, even though they dutifully state that they are overflowing with the joy of the Lord. They all know the routine of the café — when to stand, when to sit, when to give, when to sleep. They all speak English, but sometimes the dialect seems foreign. When you ask them to explain the doctrine it sounds like so many memorized words. The blue-plate special is salvation on raspberry French toast, but it's not as tasty as you would expect. It looks like a cozy cabin on the outside, but inside it feels different.

Do some people leave church after their first visit and wonder if their cholesterol can handle it? Didn't feel heart-healthy?

Taylor scored a couple of goals at the scrimmage. It was great fun hanging out with parents on the sideline. When Tay scored one of her goals, a couple of the dads yelled, "Was that Mary Esau's daughter? That Mary must have been quite the athlete!" Some of the dads mistakenly think they've got a sense of humor. I won't mention any names — Gene, Keith, Van.

We have a lot of great parents who come to every game. It's a big part of our lives. I suppose, in a way, it's pathetic, but we're okay with that. We're not particularly "happenin'" people.

Bill "The Lung" Marshall, one of the dads, is the most gifted cheerleader of the bunch. He doesn't have pom-poms or anything, thank goodness, but this man can yell louder than any human on the face of the earth. If you're within ten feet of him when he lets one fly, you lose 50 percent of your hearing. Five feet? You're deaf for a day. If you're sitting directly in front of him, you might as well paint white faces on birds, they'll be mimes to you from now on. The girls, however, from a safe distance of fifty yards, love to hear Bill cheer. He's a buck-twenty decibel encourager.

After the scrimmage we took the girls to Panera for lunch. They flirted with the guy taking our order — Sam. Even though we got our food right away, Courtney asked if he would call out her name over the sound system. He made a big deal of it. "Yeah, uh, Court-ney, your order is rrrready!" She smiled and said, "Yyyyesss."

I guess we all like to hear our names. Makes us feel like someone knows us, that we exist, we're popular. We should use each other's names whenever we can. Instead of just saying "hi" when we pass someone, we should say, "Hi Sarah Sawyer Smith," or whatever. It says to them, "I know you." And they go, "Hmm, I'm known." It's a good thing.

I came home and fell asleep for a few minutes watching the Olympics. I sound old, don't I? Got an e-mail from NavPress that said they'll call on Monday. Did some busy-work online. Mary works till eight, so I'm flying solo tonight. I don't mind so much when she's working during the day, but when she's working at night, and especially a weekend night, I miss her. I was hoping God would surprise me with a phone call from a friend saying, "Hey, I was just thinking about you and wondering if you'd want to go to a movie tonight." Didn't happen. I called a few friends looking for a movie partner, but everyone was either busy or out.

Have I mentioned my daughters think it's the ultimate in loserdom to go to a movie by yourself? "Pathetic" I believe is the word they used. Then call me pathetic: I went to see I, Robot. It was one of those "robots take over the world" stories. It raised some interesting questions about control—who and what we give it to. Do we grant too much power to things or concepts that don't deserve them? That was a rhetorical question.

I came home and Mary was already heading for bed. She always apologizes for having to go to bed early. There's no need for that. If I had to get up at 4:30 I'd be hitting the hay too.

I feel badly for her. She's missing out on a lot. Her plan is to quit this job in about two weeks. I'm glad. She's too tired. It's not really about the family suffering, it's more that she's being robbed of the last few, important activity-filled years with Taylor. I would hate that. And I hate that Mary is missing it.

Quitting will be good.

Okay, part of my, oh, let's call it unbridled happiness in Mary's decision to quit her job, has nothing to do with Taylor. No, it's about me.

Here we go again.

I don't really think this is selfish on my part. No, really. I just want to be with her. And have her with me. We're best friends and she always tops the list of who I want to spend an evening with. She's my buddy, my lover, my main squeeze. I just want more of her. I always have.

I remember when Mary and I started dating. We'd been going out for about two or three months when I called and said, "I'll pick you up at seven and . . ." She interrupted me and let me know that she couldn't go out because, well, she had a date with another guy, an old boyfriend. He meant nothing to her, she assured me.

That was an I, Robot night. I wanted to be with Mary Ann Soholt more than anything, but I was stuck with Myself. I was falling in love with her, and the thought of some other guy looking into her killer blue eyes, well, it was killing me.

I did a lot of thinking that night about us. Was some other robot, who "meant nothing to her," taking over the world, my world? How could that happen? I made some decisions that night — I would be like Will Smith in the movie. Well actually, Will Smith was more into saving the world than the damsel, so I decided I would be like a different Will — Will Parker.

Remember him as the love-struck cowboy in the musical Oklahoma? He was the guy falling for a little trollop named Ado Annie. It turns out Ado Annie had a "thing" for anything in chaps; all the cowboys coming in off the trail looked pretty good to her. I'm not saying that Mary was loosy-goosy with all the cowboys in Minneapolis, but what I am saying is that this punk c-boy who "meant nothing to her" and a certain wrangler named Esau were headed for a showdown. Fisticuffs. Two pistols and ten paces.

I knew I had to do something. I wasn't going to let Mary get away. That was a given. Not without a fight . . . or maybe a song.

I called Mary and said, "Meet me on the front lawn in ten minutes. I want to talk." She did. I sat her down, cleared my throat, and, uh, started singing. It was the song Will Parker sang to Ado Annie in *Oklahoma* when he was pleading his case, telling her that he loved her and didn't want to share her. I sang:

With me it's all or nothing
Is it all or nothing with you
You can't be in between
You can't be now and then
No half-and-half romance will do

I finished. She looked at me. Secretly, I think she was trying to keep from laughing. If I recall correctly, she said something like, "Okay," which, as it turns out, meant she was going to dump the punk c-boy who "meant nothing to her." Yippee kiyaa!

That was a surprisingly good day, a big day in the history of us. Maybe it was the beginning of us.

Oh, what a beautiful morning it was, when a few years later on June 30 we got married. We said our vows to each other, which basically were a variation of the "All or Nothing" song, and we've been watching the wind go whistling down the plain ever since. She hasn't given Judd, the punk c-boy, a second look since that day. (I like to pretend that her old boyfriend's name was Judd so I can sing, "Poor Judd is dead, poor Judd Fry is dead." I've gone too far now, haven't I?)

I can't even remember now how all this started. Oh yeah, she's quitting her job so I get more time with my baby. Life is good. I walked the mutt and called it a day. Stars were everywhere.

Oh, what a beautiful evening.

DAY TWENTY-EIGHT: A LOVE SUPREME

So yesterday I told you about the whole "All or Nothin'" fiasco. Odd, huh? Well this got me thinking about our love interest in God. Here's how I think it looks. See if you agree.

God fell in love with me—go figure. There's no explaining his taste. Just the same, we started dating. I found him to be pretty interesting, fascinating, and more real than the other gods. He's not as high-maintenance as other gods either. The others want you to jump through hoops a certain way, at certain times, while spinning plates and juggling balls—and if you do everything just so, then there's an outside chance that you might earn their love and acceptance.

My God never asked me to earn anything. In fact, he said I couldn't, I'm not capable of earning his love. Even if I dedicated my whole life to the task, bought him lots of jewelry and flowers, I still couldn't pull it off.

But—it turns out he wants me. This is a hard thing to convince myself of at times, but more and more I'm coming to believe it's true. He loves me whether I say the right things or not. He loves me whether I do the right things or not. Shoot, he loves me whether I love him or not. It's crazy.

He's simply saying, "I love you. And I think once you get to know me, you're going to love me too. Give me that chance."

In spite of his offer of love, I still find other gods to date. Work, money, success, accomplishment, recognition. And the all-time dumbest god I date is, well—me. A couple of days ago I told you about my selfish streak and the whole Mart, Texas, Postmaster incident. My preoccupation with

174

me is tantamount to dating myself. Told you I was sick. I think that is the one thing that really hurts God. Luckily he's not like me, entertaining the idea of two pistols and ten paces.

Ever since I sang that *Oklahoma* song to Mary, I keep hearing it sung to me. Not by Mary, but by — well, God. He sings it softly, more earnestly than I did for Mary. He sings:

With me it's all or nothing
Is it all or nothing with you
You can't be in between
You can't be now and then
No half-and-half romance will do

Each time he sings this song to me, I discover more and more that he's not asking me to earn his love, but asking me to put myself in a position to receive it. An un-received kiss is never felt. And we'll never feel the kiss of God if we're dating Judd and whoever else happens to be the hot god du jour.

What God is asking for is monogamy. He's saying, "Cut Judd loose. I'm your man, always have been, always will be." And he's not being selfish, just like I don't think I was when I said I just wanted more time with Mary. I just want to be with her because I love her. Same deal with God.

When I wake up every day and say, "Surprise Me, God," maybe the biggest, most unbelievable, most beautiful, most life-giving surprise of all is that the brilliant Creator of this universe loves me. When that surprise sinks in, all the way, life will never be the same. I suspect that's when the real surprises kick in.

Well it's Sunday, so I went to church — by myself. In spite of my company, church was fun. Our pastor and senior high leader talked about raising teenagers. Turns out they didn't really have any fail-proof answers either. I feel better about that. They did present a formula though: Time + Space = Change. I guess it makes sense, it's just that I'm not a big believer in formulas these days. At least not when it comes to real change in humans.

After church I had an hour to kill before I had to pick Tay up from her senior high deal. Starbucks was made for hour-killing. While there, I picked up a newspaper that was sitting on a table—the *Chicago Tribune*. Not sure how it got there, but I scanned it. In the arts section, there was a story on John Coltrane, the great jazz saxophonist. It was all about his watershed piece called "A Love Supreme." I had just bought this CD—a version that included older, newly discovered live recordings. Coltrane led a pretty tormented life, but he persevered and eventually came to a deep spiritual understanding that seeped into his music. He felt compelled to write this piece and characterized it as his tribute of praise to God. It's still considered his masterpiece.

You should all go buy this, turn the lights off, crank it up and feel one man's ultimate expression of worship. It's not exactly the praise and worship music you're probably used to, but that might be a good thing.

When I picked Tay up from church, she saw the empty plastic cup of a Vanilla Bean Frappacino, so of course she wanted one. And I'm nothing if not a total pushover. Yes, we went, she ordered, I paid, she slurped. We talked about life and stuff. I love talking about life and stuff with Tay. She makes me think differently about those two things.

Then a few friends picked her up and they were off to the Mall of America. They wanted to try a new amusement park ride, and some guy-friends of theirs wanted the girls to help them clothes shop for fall. Guys shouldn't give girls that much power so early on; it's a bad precedent.

So, here I am again, left with my shadow-twin, Myself, to kill the afternoon.

I think I'll go for a bike ride—an even better time-killer than Starbucks.

A mile into the ride I saw a guy on a time trial bike go flying by on a cross street. I proceeded to kill myself chasing down that rabbit. We rode together for about ten miles. He's racing in an Iron Man competition in Canada next weekend. He was strong. I think he could have dropped me if he had half a mind to. Lucky for me he only had a quarter mind to.

Then I met up with Gary and we rode till we came across a guy who had a flat tire. We helped him change it. Little did we know that we would have to do it again in an hour. We were cruising about 30 mph with Gary about a foot off my back wheel, when I swerved to miss a big pothole. I didn't give Gary enough warning and his front wheel dove in. Blowout. We had lots of practice changing tires today.

Got home and I grilled teriyaki chicken with a guy named Myself. Luckily we have very similar taste in food, so the food was done just the way we both like it. Broiled potatoes. Fresh raspberries. Leinie's HoneyWeiss. Watched Olympic swimming while I ate.

Tay called and asked me to pick her up. I don't have to hang out with Myself anymore. Good. Picked up Chase on the way. They came over and watched *Zoolander* while I've been writing this. So if this journal entry seems a little odd, I blame the distractions. Adam came over too. After the movie they sat in a circle talking. I plopped into the circle and said I was joining the circle of trust, the nest. The guys were okay with it; Tay kept asking if there were other things I needed to be doing. I said no. But I left before the joke got even older.

Mary just got home. She's going to Washington DC in the morning with her parents, so she's packing. They're going to see the newly opened

WWII Memorial. Mary's dad served in the war, so I'm sure it will be a meaningful time for them.

Bri is going with them, Lauren is at Baylor, Taylor, well, Taylor has such a busy social calendar that I'll rarely see her, so you know what that means: I get to spend more time with Myself.

Yippee skippie.

DAY TWENTY-NINE: FOUR GUYS

Mary and Bri headed for the airport at eight this morning for Washington DC. I've already heard from them and they're having fun — so all of you reading this don't need to worry about that. Okay?

I took my Tator Tot to soccer practice at nine. Now I'm home and doing some reading. A little Bible, then finished up with a chapter of *New Way to Be Human*. I haven't read from this in about two weeks.

Okay, what's this mean? The next chapter in *New Way to Be Human* by Charlie Peacock is all about John Coltrane's musical masterpiece "A Love Supreme." Remember, I came across an article concerning this in the *Chicago Tribune* yesterday at Starbucks. Weird. So after I finished reading the chapter and tossing out the Surprise Me prayer for the day, I decided to sit down and listen to the suite. I slapped on the headphones figuring there would be fewer interruptions. (Although I am starting to view interruptions a bit differently now.)

I had listened to the first two movements when I saw the light on the phone blinking at me. I answered — it was NavPress. They gave me more encouraging words, asked a few questions, and told me that tomorrow is the big board meeting that could decide the fate of Surprise Me (which you already know because you're reading from a book published by NavPress — but don't tell *me* yet, I want to be surprised). I sent an e-mail to my family and small group asking for their prayers.

Taylor called; soccer practice was over. She needed to eat an early lunch because she had to be back in an hour for a sports psychology session. Now there's something we didn't have in my sporting days. The extent of our psychology was when the coach said "jump," we said "how high?" Actually, we didn't say "how high," we just jumped and hoped our vertical was sufficient to his demands. Nobody ever asked us how we felt about the coach's demands to "jump." Would we have jumped higher had we understood the psychological underpinnings of our coach's request? Doubt it.

So we went to lunch. Chinese. *Mmmm.* Buffet style, but they had a person who served at the buffet. Tay and I were trying to figure out if it was to suppress the piggish-ness in us or if they were just expressing a servant attitude.

I dropped Tay off for the team shrink session and came home to finish "A Love Supreme." I finished listening and then remembered something I had read about the last movement. Evidently, Coltrane wasn't a liner notes kind of guy. That was before Grammies were given for best liner notes. But he had not only written about how this was his musical devotion to God, but he also wrote a psalm and included it. Somebody found that in the last movement, he sort of "reads" the poetry of his psalm with his saxophone. I know that sounds weird, but go listen to it. I did. You can actually follow along with his playing of the syllables of the psalm. Pretty cool. It adds different meanings because of the inflection and pitch of the notes.

I love the suite, but what does it mean for me and this Surprise Me thing? Why did I get hit with this twice? Coincidence? Did I mention that in the paper they suggested we go out and buy one particular CD of his? Just so happens that it is the same one I bought a couple months ago. But still, what does this mean for me? I don't know. I even thought today that maybe I should fly to Chicago when John's son, Ravi, performs his father's piece for the first time. Maybe a light would blast down on me or something.

Or maybe I'm just supposed to appreciate and emulate a man and his art. Maybe I'm supposed to find *my* way of expressing worship for this Love Supreme.

If that's the case, what is my "suite for God?" What is the art that I can offer him that pulls the heart from my chest and says, "Here, I believe this is yours. Take it." I don't think it was those kitty litter commercials I did, and certainly not that Inhibitor Bolus spot.

Maybe this is it, this Surprise Me thing. Or maybe it's riding my bike and running into people who need someone to talk to. Or maybe it's just not being selfish with my wife and family. Maybe it's as simple as loving people.

Another thing I read in the Tribune article was that Coltrane had proffered a simple prayer to God when he discovered him. He simply prayed, "Let me bring happiness to people with my music." Not terribly deep, but a noble gesture. If this experiment helps people see God in a way they haven't seen him before, I suspect that will bring them a measure of happiness. If Coltrane was okay with that, I guess I should be too. So let's call Surprise Me my Opus Number One.

I got an e-mail from a friend this morning telling me about a movie he saw last night. Said I have to see it. Have to! It's called *Saved*. It's about a group of friends at a Christian high school that get their faith all tangled up in goofy religious mumbo-jumbo.

At about 6:45 I decide I'm going to go to this movie. I take off. Then the anticipated words of my sixteen-year-old hit me, "You went to a movie by yourself, again, dad? Ouch." Then she'd probably do the fake cough thing while saying, "Loser!"

I made a few phone calls and found a friend who agreed to join me, keeping me from being the lone resident of Loserville. He brought a friend, too. (Losers tend to have friends that are losers.) On the way into the theater I called my buddies who had originally recommended the

181

movie and told them to meet us at this Irish pub afterward. I said, "We're going to deconstruct this movie together." They were all over it.

Hmm. Maybe Loserville isn't my destiny—I'm moving to the 'burbs of Coolsville. (I know, I know . . . that last sentence was the exact kind of thing a loser would say.)

We see some real polar opposites in the movie. Mandy Moore plays this fanatical fundamentalist who sees Jesus as a weapon to neutralize anyone who disagrees with her and a prescription-strength sedative to appease her when the weapon doesn't work. Of course her theological sedatives and weapons don't seem to have room to cohabitate in her brain without kicking the crap out of each other, so she's not exactly the poster child for peace and love. At one point in the movie Mandy's character refuses to forgive one of her friends of a "discretion" that is evidently unpardonable. Her friend reacts by asking, "Is that how Jesus loves?" Mandy's character winds up and chucks her Bible at her friend as she yells, "don't tell me I don't love you like Jesus."

There's more symbolism here than we might care to admit.

Besides the Mandy Moore crusader, we have this, uh, Jewish girl. You heard me, a nice Jewish girl at a fundamentalist Christian high school. You're smiling, aren't you? I think we may have found our antagonist.

This girl is a piece of work—feisty, smart, angry, honest, and dead-set on bringing the Mandy Moore character down. She does a pretty good job of it too. I suspect that a lot of Christians who saw this movie felt defensive. I mean, the gloves came off early and often, so why shouldn't they be?

Well, here's why. The movie is chockfull of truth. We Christians are more like Miss Mandy "Always Right" Moore's character than we care to admit. And even those of us who aren't like that need to understand that the distorted version of what it looks like to be a Christian is what much of our culture sees.

The world thinks Jesus is a fake because we're fakes more often than not. They've come to the only logical conclusion. When our faith becomes real, rather than just looking real, then good things start to happen. Then we will no longer be Stepford Christians, but rather we will love people from our toes.

So anyhow, the movie ends and we all meet over at an Irish Pub called Claddaghs. It's me, Kevin and Drew (the guys who went to the movie with me), and Jamin and the Lugermeister (my friends who had recommended the movie). We sat down and started deconstructing the movie and our feelings about what it said and didn't say—what it screamed and what it insinuated.

As this discussion was going on I sort of drifted away for a second as I was looking around the table at the faces of these guys. I started doing a sort of mental inventory of how they came into my life and the odd circumstances surrounding that. Here's what it looks like.

Kevin. I was sitting at a Barnes and Noble one day while my wife was finishing up some shopping, you know, just killing time. Kevin walks up to me and says, "I'd like to give you this book. You don't know me but I heard you speaking somewhere and I just read this book and I think you'd really like it." Kevin doesn't work at B&N; he was just shopping. The book he handed me was Donald Miller's *Blue Like Jazz*. I've given away a dozen of them myself since then.

This was a few months ago and since then we've had lunch a few times, gone to movies, been part of thought-bending discussions and I don't know what else.

Drew. Remember me talking about meeting with Riggins, this college guy, several times during the summer? Well, every time, and I mean every time I walked into Starbucks with Riggins, we always ran into Drew. I had never met him before, but Riggins knew him. We talked about the film industry, which seemed to be a real interest of Drew's. One time I saw him reading *Mere Christianity* and we talked about that.

When I called Kevin to come see *Saved* with me tonight, he showed up with Drew. I had no idea they knew each other. When Kevin said, "Can I bring a friend along?" and he showed up with Drew, I looked at him a little funny and said, "Aren't you the guy I keep running into at Starbucks?"

The Lugermeister. I've been working on putting together a deal to turn the stories from my first book into short films. I'd like to package them with a discussion guide and offer them as a tool for small groups who are looking for a different sort of approach to generating God-based discussions. Well, a friend of mine said one day, "I know this guy named Clint (aka The Lugermeister) who is really into film and is a whiz-kid of sorts." I called him and we set up a meeting. Interestingly, it was here, at Claddaghs, right where we are tonight.

He walked in and we introduced ourselves. Then he pulled a fully written screenplay from his portfolio that was based on one of my stories from my book. We hadn't even met prior to this — and he shows up with a twenty-six-page treatment of one of my stories? I soon discovered that the Lugermeister wasn't just some eager kid with too much time on his hands; this guy is potential waiting to happen. We've worked on several projects together since then.

In fact, I'm thinking of shooting a documentary of churches and colleges and book clubs as they go through this Surprise Me experiment. I'm sure the Lugermeister will be involved in that.

And the last of the four guys, Jamin. (Yes, that's his real name.) He and the Lugermeister have been buddies since they were punks. Technically, they're still punks, compared to me anyhow. Jamin is this creative, expressive, actor kind of guy. We wrote a

bizarre monologue together a few months back, and then he delivered it brilliantly in front of his church. I have a feeling we'll be doing more of that in the future.

So that's Jamin, the Lugermeister, Kevin, and Drew. Four guys with the potential to change the world. Back at Claddaghs, I looked around the table at these four guys and wondered, "Where did they come from? How did they end up in my life? And why? Is there something the five of us are going to do together? What's God up to?" This is part of the beauty of Surprise Me and our God. He's creating and orchestrating a role for us with people we may not even know yet, doing something we haven't even thought of yet. Life with God is a surprise just waiting to happen. I love it.

Oh, and one thing all four of these guys have in common — they're all about twenty years younger than me. I'd like to hate them for that, but I guess it's not their fault.

I left them tonight and found out later that they had stayed for two more hours talking, thinking, dreaming, and questioning.

It was an interesting day. Tomorrow is the last day of the experiment. Seems weird. It feels like I just started, and yet it seems like I've been doing this forever. I'm curious what tomorrow will look like.

DAY THIRTY/AM: CONSTRUCTION BARREL

Day thirty. I guess this is it, the end of the experiment. Somehow I thought I'd have more answers by now. I was hoping for more wisdom. More clarity—some clarity. Secretly, I think I was hoping for more mind-shattering events. I guess I wanted to wow you, impress you, make you think this Terry Esau dude has it going on.

Surprise!

I'm just me. Not that deep, not that spiritual, not that impressive. Sometimes I can be as fake as those "designer" purses my daughters bought in the back alleys of Soho.

Did I make some progress in living a real, authentic faith? I think so. Did I find a God who showed up where and when he wanted to, and not always how I wanted him to? Yup. Did God find me looking for him more intentionally, more passionately? Absolutely. No question about it. Did I have fun? Heck yes!

On to the day.

Bailey and I went for a walk and we prayed, "Surprise Me, God" one last time. Well, I'm not sure Bailey prayed that, but pretty much all of life is new and surprising for that mutt. She chased a leaf, just because. She sniffed at a dragonfly and sneezed when its wings tickled her nose. She barked at some geese flying overhead. She picked just the right spot to relieve herself—this is always the biggest decision of her morning. Okay, you're right, she probably didn't pray with me this morning, but that's only because she was already too busy *being* surprised, living a life of surprise. Maybe there's a lesson there.

I headed over to church to meet with Steve about planning the kickoff Sunday for Surprise Me. The journals that everyone is going to receive on that Sunday are going to be really cool. We've got a nice cover designed, thanks to the Lugermeister. I wrote a new intro and epilogue for it. It all makes sense, I think.

Mike, the bicyclist/mountain climber, has agreed to do a live interview with me to tell the story of our ride from Day Two. (Read it again, it was a cool day.) I'm also doing a man-on-the-street video, sidewalk interviews with people from downtown — you know, just asking them questions about surprises they've had, ones they've liked, disliked. It should be a fun setup for the morning.

Then Paul, our pastor, is going to talk about how God loves to surprise us and give a bunch of illustrations from the Bible, including a time when God was surprised — by us. Luke 7. Yeah, he was surprised at the centurion's faith. Cool. We can surprise God — who knew? I like that.

We're talking about opening the morning with all the lights off and having distant thunder rumble through the auditorium — the PA system turned to eleven. Then we're going to fade 1 Corinthians 2:9 onto the screen. "No eye has seen, no ear has heard, no mind has conceived what God has prepared for those who love him." The morning will end with an invitation for everyone to come back on Wednesday nights where we'll tell these stories to each other. I left feeling very positive about what this can and will do for our church. I've got to believe that this is going to go a long way toward creating a new sense of community.

I came home to one of my last chances to have lunch with Taylor before school starts again. Two of her friends and one of the dads came with us to Black's Ford, a little sandwich place in Wayzata. We talked about boys, soccer, school, boys, clothes, friends, boys . . .

When I got home from lunch there was an e-mail from one of the publishers interested in *Surprise Me.* It said, "Aren't the thirty days almost up? Are you ready to talk?" I sent him an e-mail back that said, yes, I was ready to start talking, and I sent him one of the daily journal entries. It feels like this thing is gathering momentum. I wonder what will happen with it?

Taylor had a soccer game about fifteen miles away so I decided I would ride my bike there, watch the game then ride back—you know, kill one trip with two wheels. It was a perfect day for a ride. And what's day thirty without a ride? My favorite surprises seem to happen on my bike. Maybe again?

The trip there was uneventful, except for the ten-mile additional loop I took called "lost." Sometimes lost is a good place to visit because it makes found feel better. But lost on a bicycle is different than lost in a car. Ten miles out of the way on a bike is somehow much farther. Eventually, I rolled onto the sidelines and sat down to watch soccer, the beautiful game.

Now picture this (if you dare). I'm wearing cycling's version of rock and roll, you know, that whole spandex look. Hey, it's all about wind resistance, cut me some slack here. I'm not trying to make a fashion statement. I get lots of weird looks, but I'm used to it. My daughter isn't. It does make it easier for her to point me out to her friends, "Uh, yeah, he's the geek in the bright colored polyester." How could she not be proud?

The game is moving along just fine. My cell phone rings. It's NavPress. They've just gotten out of their editorial meeting and they want to make an offer for Surprise Me. This, without reading a word of the manuscript, my journal. I had only sent them the proposal, no content, just concept. Still, they made an offer. It's day thirty of the experiment—the last day. Doesn't that seem a bit surreal? I mean, I love the way life shuttles us around, the way God maneuvers the puzzle pieces, but this is almost too much. I started laughing. I went over to a friend, and with a nerdy grin on my face I said, "I think I just got an offer for my book." He congratulated me and said, "Nice duds, Esau." We talked awhile, the game ended, and I hopped on my bike to head home.

The game wasn't particularly successful for us. Not only did we lose, but Rachel, one of our best defenders, went down with a bad ankle sprain.

I'm back on the road, deep in thought about publishing this and that when some crazy dude started inching his car toward me. Then he laid on his horn and moved even closer. The crazy man in his red car with horn blaring finally nudged me right into an orange construction barrel and I heard him laughing as he floored it and moved on to his next victim. I nailed the barrel with my left arm and leg but managed to keep from crashing altogether. As I pulled to a stop, I did a quick self-assessment—scrape on my arm, a little blood, but nothing serious. Then I had a moment of anger. "You idiot!" I thought out loud, as in LOUD.

I didn't get his license plate number. I never do. There's no time when stuff like that happens; I'm always too busy trying to stay upright. Oh well. Let it go.

I looked up and I was right in front of a coffee shop. "Almost-accident victims deserve a treat," I thought. I pulled in, got a smoothie and a muffin. I went outside and sat down on a bench, took a bite, a drink, and a breath.

I was in my own world, the state of dazed, somewhere between publishing deals and collisions with orange barrels, when another cyclist came up to me and asked if he could share the bench. I slid over, he sat down and we started to talk. He didn't look like the typical cyclist. He was wearing street clothes—dress pants, a shirt, and—wing tipped shoes. I've never seen Lance Armstrong in wingtips on his bike.

We made small talk for a while. I told him about the lunatic assassin.

He empathized. Then he started to tell me about his father-in-law who was dying. He said, "I'm really struggling right now with how to tell my children about this. Do I tell them? I suppose I have to. I don't want them to be shocked when the inevitable happens. But how do you tell these little kids that the grandpa they love is going to die . . . soon?"

I didn't have any brilliant answers for him, but I did say that I could tell by the way he was talking to me that he would come up with the right time and the right way to tell them. He was a kind, tenderhearted guy. Those kind of guys usually figure out how to do these things.

We talked some more. I found out that his name was Norm, he was a parole officer, he worked downtown, he liked his job but sometimes it took a toll on him emotionally. That's why he was riding in his street clothes. He had his bike in his car, and on his commute home he decided he needed to release some of the day's stress, so he parked his car and was making a fifteen-mile loop.

That's what got him to The Depot coffee shop today. For me it took a sicko in a red car. Neither of us had planned a stop at The Depot, but here we were. I told him it was a nice surprise, which of course led to telling him about Surprise Me. I told him he was probably one of my last surprises since I only had a few hours left in the experiment. He was very interested in the whole thing. He gave me his card, and I said I would send him a copy of my book. We connected in a way that doesn't happen in ten minutes with strangers. Maybe it was the wingtips, I don't know. We talked a bit more and we went our separate ways.

I rode home with a great sense of peace. Unexpected, considering the orange barrel incident. But knowing the red car that led me to the orange barrel that led me to the brown Depot that led me to Norm was all part of a surprising plan — one that had been designed just for me and Norm, just for today, well, that gave me a new awareness of the big picture. It said, Norm and Terry are of great value to God. This is a humbling thing.

To think that the God of the universe can and will orchestrate space and time and physical circumstances to make sure that two of his people connect, on a day when they've got something to give each other, well, that's just amazing!

As I rode and breathed, I already was thinking of tomorrow. If this God planned some specifics for me today, it follows that he's probably planned something for my tomorrow too. And the day after that. And after that.

I poured a few more watts to the pedals without realizing it. Thinking. He's probably got some plans for me years from now. Decades.

I took the back way into our neighborhood and almost ran into our next-door neighbor who was out for a walk. I stopped and talked for a while, a long while. Remember early in the experiment how we had a fund-raiser party for my cousin from Cambodia and his wife? Well, this neighbor had been at that party and now she said they wanted to contribute a computer to Tim and Dar. Cool. They need a new computer — or two. Then she started telling me about the interesting aspect of this new "window of time" in her and her husband's life. Kids are all grown and gone. Now what? She was talking Peace Corps, missions, or maybe something else altogether. It was fun to hear her talk that way. It's always fun hearing people talk about giving their lives away. Inspiring.

The shower felt great. It always does after a long, hot, hard ride. Especially after rides where I'm fighting for my fair share of the asphalt. I'm still not sure of what "A Love Supreme" is supposed to be about.

DAY THIRTY/ PM: THREE SONGS

Tay offered to make me dinner tonight — Mac and cheese. *Mmmmm.* Don't tell me my kid can't cook. She was in a great mood. Evidently getting schooled by the Blake soccer team this afternoon was only a temporary emotional setback. Her bounce-back factor is impressive. Gotta like that.

A bunch of her friends were over for the evening so we were all just hanging out. Our house has been Party Central this month. The refrigerator gets opened and closed countless times, causing food to disappear into mouths right under our noses. The screen door gets left open allowing a mother-load of mosquitoes to enter, and our delinquent dog to depart. The carpet takes a beating — Coke, nachos, Laffy Taffy, Nerds, and worms of both the gummy and real varieties. Speakers pump, movies rumble, and laughter ricochets. Peace and Quiet are the only delinquents that don't seem to pass through our doors. We wouldn't have it any other way.

Chaos means that life is happening here. Contact is being made. Friendships are growing. For teenagers, noise is the potting soil of life. Which reminds me, there's plenty of soil in the carpet too.

So the house was jumping as Jack and Diane drove up. They wanted to know if I would join them for ice cream. Duh. Now there's a surprise that works for me. Mary was still at work, so we took off. Being the third wheel doesn't particularly bother me, and when ice cream is factored into the equation, well, I hopped into the proverbial sidecar and we were off.

We went to Adelle's. They make custard ice cream. Have you had it? If not, your T-buds have just been putting in time; they haven't discovered their true purpose in life yet. I had a chocolate raspberry truffle sundae. Oh baby, they're good!

We had a fun conversation. Jack was divorced several years ago and is re-entering the dating scene. It turns out that Jack and Diane had dated in their early twenties, then they both went on to marry other people. Now, both divorced, they ran into each other at Lunds, a grocery store. They did a double-take as they looked at each other, then reintroduced themselves. It had been over twenty years. They exchanged numbers and said good-bye. A week later my slow friend, Jack, finally made the call. Now it's been almost a year.

It's weird to see my daughter finally dating, "officially," and then to see my friend Jack also re-enter that scene. And to think how different it must be to come at dating from such disparate perspectives. For Taylor it's a whole new world of surprise and excitement. For Jack it's probably more apprehension and caution. He knows the game. He's played it before and wasn't really planning on playing it again.

This Surprise Me experiment is kind of like stepping back into the dating scene again, with God. When we first started "dating" God, it was all new and exciting. We didn't know what to expect. Everything was a first. First hand hold, first hug, first kiss. We wanted to spend time with him, because he was mysterious, interesting, and enticing. But then we grew more and more comfortable with him. That can be good and bad. Familiarity can be the predecessor of contentment, but it can also deposit us at the doorstep of apathy, especially if we think and assume that we know all there is to know about this God. You know, "I've read the book, I've heard the sermons, I've played the part — I must have this all figured out."

Apathy in our relationship with God is probably the equivalent of divorce. He has no time for low-level relational game-playing. God has little interest in casual sex-spirituality. He's interested in lovemaking of the heart.

Deep down we know there's more. Deep down we sense that God is a lover, a relational spelunker.

Remember the "All or Nothing" song I sang to Mary? The "I'd like to turn you into a one-man woman" aria? Well, without the "All or Nothing" song we'd still be casually dating. Or we'd just be acquaintances. We wouldn't be married. We wouldn't be a family. We wouldn't be in love. We wouldn't know each other intimately, personally, passionately.

We wouldn't be us. There would still be a Mary and Terry, but no us. God wanted there to be an us. And he wants there to be an us with him too. He's okay with casual dating, as long as it doesn't stay there. He wants us to question, to look him up and down. He knows that we're cautious, skeptical creatures, and that even when dating God, there is some sniffing around that needs to take place.

But he also knows that what he has to give us is not available anywhere else. Pure love is rare. He wants us to want him, not so much because he needs us, but because he knows we need him. He's the ultimate mystery man who can help us to unwrap the mystery that is us.

I challenged Mary to make a decision all those years ago, and I offered a commitment to go along with that. God does the same with us. And then he makes a commitment, a pretty dang good one. "Nothing can separate us from the love of God. Neither height nor depth, neither things above or below, neither things seen or unseen . . . nothing can separate us from the love of God."

It was around eleven o'clock when Peace and Quiet, those disingenuous vagabond cousins of mine, finally stopped in to pay a short, overdue visit. The ringing in my ears was downgraded to a twenty-decibel hum. That's one of my favorite things about night. There is almost an imposed sense of peace that filters down on our street, our yard, our house.

I snapped Bailey onto her leash and we walked out into that quiet darkness. It was the final hour of my thirty-day experiment. The same stars were twinkling that had been there a month ago. The same street, the same houses, the same trees, the same smells, sounds, and breeze. If my neighbors had been looking out their windows, they wouldn't have been able to distinguish this night from the one thirty nights ago.

But something was different. Or someone.

Me.

It was the same body (slightly older) walking Bailey, but my perspective had changed. Now the stars twinkled with mystery, the road was a pathway to the unexpected, and the breeze was a courier of surprises. Everything was ripe with potential. Everything was charged with the possibility of being an agent of God's surprise. To quote Peter Mayer's song, "everything was holy now." God hadn't changed, and maybe I could argue that my life hadn't really changed. But now I saw God and what he was doing in my life. Now, I was regularly peeking up his sleeve — and he's got an armful of surprises living up there.

Here's my take on it: God is constantly up to something. And here's the important part, he's up to something *with me*.

He's shown me that I can be his sidekick. He's written me into the script. I am a chosen partner of his. I am the Starsky to his Hutch. He gets a call on his two-way radio, and we're off in his Gran Torino to intervene in some incident. I am the Paul Shaffer to his David Letterman. He lets me be the straight man to his jokes — and then I get to laugh with him. I am the Max Weinberg to his Conan O'Brien. He lets me accompany him and create the mood for his show. I am the fork to his knife. He lets me hold the meat while he makes the cuts. I am the sock to his shoe, the spring to his step. The glove to his hand, the touch to his feel.

I am the Terry to his God.

I'm sure you've heard of us. We're big around here. I'm kidding—and yet in a way, I'm not. Here's why. If and when we partner up with God, our immediate world, our sphere of influence will be permanently and significantly affected by that partnership. The lonely will be befriended, the hurting will be held, the accused will be given grace, the poor will receive unexpected gifts.

People will get loved.

When people see me do these things, they will say, "That's not our Terry. Isn't he more selfish than that? He must be partnering up with somebody. Who's his sidekick, anyway? Must be one incredible dude!" And they'll be right. And people will hear about us. And we'll be big around here, because what they will see will not be normal. Especially not normal for me.

So, yeah, it's the same stars, road, and breeze, but this Surprise Me thing has opened my eyes to the potential of the God/Me partnership. I see now what was probably always there. And now that I see what he's up to, I am more likely to choose to engage, to hop in the Torino and say, "Floor this red rocket and let's see what this hemi can do."

I think what happened with this Surprise Me thing is that it got me looking up again.

Bailey and I turned around at the end of the block. I looked upward and asked, "Anything else? You're down to your last half-hour—anything else you want to throw at me?"

Silence.

There are so many unfinished stories from these thirty days. So many endings that needed to be written.

But all I heard was silence. Peace. Quiet.

It seemed like God was saying, "Don't worry, there's more to come in the morning, but for now, go, sleep, rest. This was enough for today. Enough for thirty days. The experiment may be over, but I'm not done. And neither are you. We're still partners. The Torino is in the garage for tonight, but tomorrow we'll fire that thing up again and we'll ride. You and me, partner."

How lucky am I? I get to ride with God, the Creator-of-the-universe-God. I get to be about his work. I get to play a role in his drama. How lucky I am!

I climbed into bed. Too many thoughts were still swirling. Before long I heard Mary's deep breathing.

I was struck by a sadness. I'm not sure I want this to end. It's been fun, exciting, energizing. Maybe I should make it 40 days. Or 60.

As I lay there, unable to corner unconsciousness, I started humming that dang song once in my life, while I was sitting on the toilet at a Cracker Barrel in Waco Texas, no less. And it haunts me, stalks me.

You're just window shopping
Window shopping
You're only looking around
You're not buying
You're just trying
Looking for the best deal in town

My thirty-day experiment is going to end with this? How wrong is that?

Then the other theme song of my thirty days came back to me. "A Love Supreme."

A love supreme
A love supreme
A love supreme

Okay God, what the heck do these two songs have to do with each other, with this experiment, with me, with life? Just let me go to sleep. Please.

I started thinking about day one of the experiment, the fleece thing. Was I testing God or was he testing me? Then I thought about Mary—Sleeping Beauty doing her heavy breathing next to me in bed. I looked at her, so still and peaceful, and beautiful. I love that woman. I have ever since the day I sang that goofy song to her. "With me it's all or nothin,' is it all or nothin' with you?" Hmmm, maybe there are three theme songs for this Surprise Me experiment.

Maybe these three songs are a sequence. I did a lot of window shopping when I was in college. A lot of trying and no buying. Until I saw Mary in the window of Cartier. Then my tune changed. I realized I was done shopping. And I didn't want anybody else to look at her and think they could put her in their cart and head off to the checkout line. So, I sang "With Me It's All Or Nothin.'" And now, twenty-six years later, we're walking around with "A Love Supreme," well, some days we are anyhow.

There was a progression. From nothing to something, from acquaintance to lover, from stranger to partner.

God has a huge karaoke machine up in heaven, and he's got those same three songs cued up. He sings them to all of us. When we hear him singing to us, we look up and say, "Hey, the big guy is singing to me. Cool." Then we start making choices. Do we want to continue dating around, trying but not buying? He sings a little more. He's pretty enticing, so we date him, regularly but not exclusively. One day he asks us to meet him in a neighbor's yard and he sings "With me, it's all or nothing. Is it all or nothing with you? You can't be in-between. You can't be now and then. No half and half romance will do."

His love for us is complete and perfect, and maybe even a little jealous. One day we realize that we'll never find a love like this anywhere else. We look up and start mirroring his moves, reading his lips, memorizing the tune coming from his mouth. We hear strains of "A Love Supreme." We sing along. We know this is where we were meant to be, meant to live. The Torino pulls into our driveway and we hop in, shotgun, with our partner. Our partner, the God of heaven and earth. Our partner, the Creator of the universe. Our partner, the only one who knows us completely and loves us perfectly.

This is the biggest surprise of all, the natural conclusion to this Surprise Me experiment: God loves us so much that he wants to spend his days with us. Not just eternity, but today and tomorrow and the next day. Not just watching us, but walking with us. Not just observing us, but engaging with us. Not just Sundays, but every day. Not just hand-holding, but love-making.

I fall asleep, a fleece that has been soaked in holy water. A fleece that knows it belongs. A fleece that has been loved for thirty days, and there's no end in sight.

AUTHOR

Terry Esau built a career in the ad business creating musical spots for everyone from McDonalds to Target, Harleys to Hondas, Pepsi to Perkins. He pedaled everything from Golden Grahams to the "Place for fun in your life — Mall of America." Then, one day he woke up with seller's remorse. "I've promoted a lot of products that *improve* people's lives, but nothing that really *changes* them."

That's when he got proactive. He wrote a book called *Blue Collar God/White Collar God*. He started telling stories about the one thing that he knew could *change* people's lives — a relationship with God. He knew because it changed his life.

Now he's taking this story on the road. The *Surprise Me Experiment* is rolling out to churches, college campuses, and groups of every kind across America. Terry spends much of his time traveling and speaking to audiences, encouraging this life of adventure and surprise.

Terry and his wife, Mary, have three daughters and live in Minneapolis, Minnesota.

THE WEBSITE

For more info on *Surprise Me* happenings, conferences, events, and experiments in your area, visit the web site at: www.surprisemegod.com.

DO THE EXPERIMENT WITH YOUR GROUP

To do the *Surprise Me* Experiment with your small group, church, college, high school, men's group, or women's group, go to the website to find materials, guides, and helpful hints.

THE BLOG/FORUM

Tell your stories to each other and discuss the concepts in the book at www.surprisemegod.com. Set up a separate link for your own group.

THE DOCUMENTARY & VIDEO LECTURE SERIES

To see excerpts of the documentary based on this *Surprise Me* Experiment, or to order copies of the Documentary or Video Lecture Series on DVD, visit the website. These DVDs are a must-have tool if your group is planning to do the experiment.

TO BOOK TERRY FOR SPEAKING ENGAGEMENTS

Visit: www.surprisemegod.com.

CONTACT TERRY

E-mail: terry@surprisemegod.com

Phone: 952-476-2204

OTHER BOOKS BY TERRY ESAU

Blue Collar God/White Collar God —
Available at www.surprisemegod.com